STRONG MEN IN TOUGH TIMES

BEING A HERO IN CULTURAL CHAOS

MAJORING IN MEN®
The Curriculum for Men

Edwin Louis Cole

RESOLUTE BOOKS

Southlake, Texas

STRONG MEN IN TOUGH TIMES WORKBOOK :
Being a Hero in Cultural Chaos

Christian Men's Network
P.O. Box 93478
Southlake, TX 76092
www.ChristianMensNetwork.com

Facebook.com/EdwinLouisCole

ISBN: 978-1-93862-916-7
Printed in the United States of America
© 2014 Edwin and Nancy Cole Legacy LLC

Published by:
Resolute Books™
1030 Hunt Valley Circle
New Kensington, PA 15068

1 2 3 4 5 6 7 8 9 10 11 / 20 19 18 17 16 15 14

TABLE OF CONTENTS

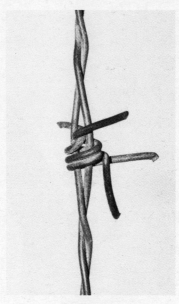

Lesson 1

The Challenge

Lesson 1
The Challenge

A. Read Daniel 1.

1. God created men to be _____ and _____. *(page 10)*

2. Some things are more important than life itself. *(page 10)* ____ True ____ False

3. What are some traits of good fathers who try to motivate their children to be good citizens? *(page 11)*

   a. _____ the laws b. exhibit _____ c. behave _____

4. Choose words from the list below to answer the following questions: *(pages 11-12)*
   moral fiber   morally   resistance   technologically   spiritually   goodness

   a. In what way is today's world progressing? _____

   b. In what ways is today's world regressing? _____ and _____

   c. What do the wicked hate? _____

   d. Where is a man's strength found? _____

   e. By what standard is strength measured? _____

For Further Study

Men as godly leaders – *"Must manage his own family well and see that his children obey him with proper respect ... must manage his children and his household well"* 1 Timothy 3:4, 12 NIV

God commands man to take dominion over all of the earth – Genesis 1:26-28.

Obey government powers we are under – Romans 13:1-7; Titus 3:1; 1 Peter 2:13-17

Integrity – *"The just man walketh in his integrity"* Proverbs 20:7.

Honesty is the core of integrity – Proverbs 11:3, 5.

B.   The Strength

    1.   A man's inner strength determines if he'll be able to withstand temptation. *(page 12)*

       ____ True   ____ False

    2.   What is a man to produce? *(circle one)* *(pages 12-13)*

       a. children   b. good work   c. manhood

    3.   We must regain the spirit of manhood in _____ and _____,

       the power of manhood in _____ and _____,

       and the conviction of manhood in _____ and moral _____.

       (page 14)

For Further Study

Truth is not an option in life – Zechariah 8:16. Truth is the bedrock of integrity. Your personal integrity is the cornerstone of your character – Psalm 24:4, 5. You receive God's own goodness as your blessing from Him, planted in your life by God Himself, your Savior.

Moral courage enables a person to encounter hatred, disapproval and contempt without departing from what is right – Psalm 119:157. Examples: Gideon – Judges 6, 7; David – 1 Samuel 17; Daniel – Daniel 6; John the Baptist – Matthew 14:3-10; Stephen – Acts 7; Paul – Acts 27; 28:1-6.

Keeping your word to spiritual leadership – *"I assure you, most solemnly I tell you, he who receives and welcomes and takes into his heart any messenger of Mine receives Me [in just that way]; and he who receives and welcomes and takes Me into his heart receives Him Who sent Me [in that same way]"* John 13:20 AMP; Acts 5:3, 4.

God holds us accountable for our words – Matthew 12:36.

A man's name is only as good as his word – *"A good man is known by his truthfulness; a false man by deceit and lies"* Proverbs 12:17 TLB; *"A good name is rather to be chosen than great riches, and loving favour rather than silver and gold"* Proverbs 22:1.

C. The Model

1. Today is a time for _____. *(page 17)*

2. Daniel was a man with Christlike qualities. What were some of Daniel's attributes? *(page 17)*

    a. Unashamed _____   e. _____ faith

    b. _____ standard   f. Unusual _____

    c. _____ protection   g. _____ blessing

    d. Unhindered _____   h. _____ influence

3. Read aloud: *"Just as my mouth can taste good food, so my mind tastes truth when I hear it"* Job 12:11 TLB.

4. Men today must acquire a _____ if they want to maximize their manhood. *(page 18)*

5. Men without an organized system of thought will always _____

    _____. *(page 18)*

For Further Study

Excellence in spirit – *"Then this Daniel was preferred above the presidents and princes, because an excellent spirit was in him; and the king thought to set him over the whole realm"* Daniel 6:3.

It takes courage to resist peer pressure and dare to be different – Psalm 119:51, 52; Daniel 1:8. It takes courage to submit to righteousness – Psalm 119:30; It takes courage to say "No" – *"I have refrained my feet from every evil way, that I might keep thy word"* Psalm 119:101; It takes courage to admit a desire to be a man of God – *"Depart from me, ye evildoers: for I will keep the commandments of my God"* Psalm 119:115; *"Choosing rather to suffer affliction with the people of God, than to enjoy the pleasures of sin for a season"* Hebrews 11:25.

Be honest with God – *"Behold, thou desirest truth in the inward parts: and in the hidden part thou shalt make me to know wisdom"* Psalm 51:6; *"O Lord, thou hast searched me, and known me. Thou knowest my downsitting and mine uprising, thou understandest my thought afar off ... Whither shall I go from thy spirit? or whither shall I flee from thy presence?"* Psalm 139:1-7; *"Neither is there any creature that is not manifest in his sight: but all things are naked and opened unto the eyes of him with whom we have to do"* Hebrews 4:13.

D. The Call

1. Nolan Ryan, the great American baseball player, had greatness due to what? *(page 19)*

_____

_____

2. The lowest level of knowledge is _____. Just above that is

_____. Then _____ then

_____ then _____ and finally _____. *(page 19)*

3. The greatest of men discipline themselves to _____. *(page 19)*

4. Why was Daniel's message so credible? *(page 20)* _____

For Further Study

Character is built in private. It develops out of a lifetime of individual decisions which either enhance or diminish it – *"I have chosen the way of truth: thy judgments have I laid before me"* Psalm 119:30; *"If a man therefore purge himself from these, he shall be a vessel unto honour, sanctified, and meet for the master's use, and prepared unto every good work"* 2 Timothy 2:21.

The result of prayer in private is a life of boldness and courage in public. *"And when they had prayed … they spake the word of God with boldness"* Acts 4:31.

Become wise – *"Every prudent man acts out of knowledge, but a fool exposes his folly"* Proverbs 13:16 NIV; *"O ye simple, understand wisdom: and, ye fools, be ye of an understanding heart"* Proverbs 8:5.

"For the Lord grants wisdom! His every word is a treasure of knowledge and understanding" Proverbs 2:6 TLB.

Knowledge – You must know right from wrong to know what to resist or accept – Psalm 119:104.

5. Why is the man always more important than the message? *(page 20)*

   _____

   _____

6. The goal of our lives is not to live life to the maximum, but to _____

   _____. *(page 20)*

7. _____ can come in a _____, but _____

   comes with _____. *(page 20)*

8. What is a good definition of a "hero"? *(page 20)*

   _____

   _____

For Further Study

False prophets – *"Then the Lord said unto me, The prophets prophesy lies in my name: I sent them not, neither have I commanded them, neither spake unto them: they prophesy unto you a false vision and divination, and a thing of nought, and the deceit of their heart"* Jeremiah 14:14; *"Beware of false prophets, which come to you in sheep's clothing, but inwardly they are ravening wolves"* Matthew 7:15; *"For there shall arise false Christs, and false prophets, and shall show great signs and wonders; insomuch that, if it were possible, they shall deceive the very elect"* Matthew 24:24.

God's fullness – *"And to know the love of Christ, which passeth knowledge, that ye might be filled with all the fulness of God"* Ephesians 3:19; *"Till we all come in the unity of the faith, and of the knowledge of the Son of God, unto a perfect man, unto the measure of the stature of the fulness of Christ"* Ephesians 4:13

Recognize that, as a man, you were created by God to be successful – a hero and a champion – Genesis 1:26.

Practical:

1. How is the world different today from when you were a child? _____

    _____

    _____

2. **In your own words,** what is the world looking for? _____

    _____

3. What is the dream you would like to attain to? _____

    _____

4. What set Daniel apart from others? In what areas are you like him? In what areas do you need work?

    _____

    _____

    _____

Repeat this prayer out loud:

Father, in Jesus' Name, I want to be a man with the spirit of a Daniel. I want to stand for right and righteousness. Please help me through this study to become more conformed to the image of Christ, which I know is the very image of a real man. Thank You. Amen.

For Further Study

Recognize your gifts, talents and abilities, and dedicate them to God – Romans 12:1.

Let God put creative ideas in your mind and godly desires in your heart – Psalm 37:4. Let Him fulfill His will by enabling you to realize those dreams.

"For I know the thoughts and plans that I have for you, says the Lord, thoughts and plans for welfare and peace and not for evil, to give you hope in your final outcome" Jeremiah 29:11 AMP.

Self Test *Lesson 1*

1. Did God create men to be leaders and heroes?   ____ Yes   ____ No

2. What is your definition of "martyrdom"? _____
    _____

3. What things in your life are more important to you than "life itself"? _____
    _____

4. Strength is proven by how it reacts to _____.

5. God created all living creatures to produce after their own kind.
    Use these words to fill in the blanks below: Oysters   Men   Plants

    a. _____ produce fruits.   b. _____ produce pearls.   c. _____ produce manhood.

6. For men to be men again, they must regain the spirit of manhood in _____ and
    _____, the power of manhood in _____ and
    _____ and the conviction of manhood in _____ and
    moral _____.

7. Men without an organized system of thought will always be what? *(circle one)*

    a. at the mercy of men who have one   b. poor students

8. The lowest level of knowledge is assumption.   ____ True   ____ False

9. It is true. Fame can come in a _____, but _____ comes
    with _____.

10. Heroes are men who act in a moment of time on a _____.

Keep this test for your own records.

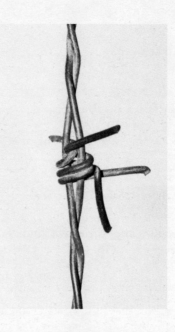

Lesson 2
The Ultimate Decision

Lesson 2
The Ultimate Decision

A. Read Daniel 2.

    1. When Daniel's enemies were unable to discover a flaw, they did what? *(circle one)* *(page 23)*

        a. sabotaged him   b. used his strength as a weakness   c. left him alone

    2. Read: *"But Daniel purposed in his heart that he would not defile himself with the portion of the king's meat, nor with the wine which he drank: therefore he requested of the prince of the eunuchs that he might not defile himself"* Daniel 1:8.

       What was the first thing Daniel did? *(circle one)* *(page 24)*

        a. ate a good meal   b. purposed in his heart   c. requested of the prince

    3. An _____, _____ heart gives great strength of mission. *(page 24)*

    4. Perseverance will always outlast _____. *(page 25)*

B. The Importance of Believing

    1. A person's belief system holds or creates what? *(circle one)* *(page 26)*

        a. the greatest potential for good or harm in life   b. his choice of entertainment

---

For Further Study

A purposed heart – *"Thou hast proved mine heart; thou hast visited me in the night; thou hast tried me, and shalt find nothing; I am purposed that my mouth shall not transgress"* Psalm 17:3.

Be established in Him – *"He brought me up also out of an horrible pit, out of the miry clay, and set my feet upon a rock, and established my goings"* Psalm 40:2; *"His heart is established, he shall not be afraid, until he see his desire upon his enemies"* Psalm 112:8; *"Ponder the path of thy feet, and let all thy ways be established"* Proverbs 4:26; *"A man shall not be established by wickedness: but the root of the righteous shall not be moved"* Proverbs 12:3.

Agreement produces power – *"And the Lord said, Behold, they are one people, and they have all one language; and this is only the beginning of what they will do, and now nothing they have imagined they can do will be impossible for them"* Genesis 11:6 AMP; Exodus 13:18; Amos 3:3; *"If two of you shall agree on earth as touching any thing that they shall ask, it shall be done for them of my Father which is in heaven"* Matthew 18:19.

2. To believe in the positive, men must discipline themselves away from what? *(circle one)* *(page 27)*

    a. sin   b. faulty motivational speakers   c. the negative of the world

3. Circle the five common denominators in financially successful men. *(page 27)*

    a. intelligence   f. communication skills

    b. good luck   g. experience

    c. a positive attitude   h. highly networked

    d. financial backing   i. leveraged

    e. integrity

4. Belief is the basis for conduct, _____ and _____. *(page 28)*

C. Faith and Fear

1. Faith and fear are both extensions of _____. *(fill in the blank)* *(page 29)*

    emotions   your personality   belief

2. Faith and fear are both defined as what? *(circle one)* *(page 29)*

    a. emotions that run away with you   b. that what you cannot see will come to pass

---

For Further Study

Think right – *"Finally, brethren, whatsoever things are true, whatsoever things are honest, whatsoever things are just, whatsoever things are pure, whatsoever things are lovely, whatsoever things are of good report; if there be any virtue, and if there be any praise, think on these things"* Philippians 4:8; *"For as he thinketh in his heart, so is he: Eat and drink, saith he to thee; but his heart is not with thee"* Proverbs 23:7.

God's Word is the source of faith – *"Man shall not live by bread alone, but by every word that proceedeth out of the mouth of God"* Matthew 4:4; Psalm 119:12, 105.

Exercise faith, not fear – *"Now faith is the substance of things hoped for, the evidence of things not seen"* Hebrews 11:1; *"For God hath not given us the spirit of fear; but of power, and of love, and of a sound mind"* 2 Timothy 1:7; *"The wicked flee when no man pursueth: but the righteous are bold as a lion"* Proverbs 28:1; Genesis 3:10; *"There is no fear in love; but perfect love casteth out fear: because fear hath torment"* 1 John 4:18.

3. Faith attracts the _____. *(page 29)*

4. Fear attracts the _____. *(page 29)*

5. _____ is the most expensive commodity in life. *(page 29)*

6. Read: *"Take My yoke upon you and learn from Me, for I am gentle and humble in heart, and you will find rest for your souls. For My yoke is easy and My burden is light"* Matthew 11:29-30 NASB.

    List some things people are "yoked" to. *(page 31)* _____

    _____

    _____

    _____

7. Whatever God authors, He will _____. *(page 32)*

D. Choices Have Consequences

    1. Choices determine _____. *(page 33)*

    2. Why do some men miss opportunities? *(page 33)*

    _____

    _____

For Further Study

Submitting to God's yoke – Matthew 11:28, 29; *"And it shall come to pass in that day, that his burden shall be taken away from off thy shoulder, and his yoke from off thy neck, and the yoke shall be destroyed because of the anointing"* Isaiah 10:27; *"Being then made free from sin, ye became the servants of righteousness"* Romans 6:18; *"Be ye not unequally yoked together with unbelievers: for what fellowship hath righteousness with unrighteousness? and what communion hath light with darkness?"* 2 Corinthians 6:14; *"Stand fast therefore in the liberty wherewith Christ hath made us free, and be not entangled again with the yoke of bondage"* Galatians 5:1. Complete in Christ – *"And ye are complete in him, which is the head of all principality and power"* Colossians 2:10; *"Looking unto Jesus the author and finisher of our faith; who for the joy that was set before him endured the cross, despising the shame, and is set down at the right hand of the throne of God"* Hebrews 12:2.

3. Circle the best prayer. *(page 33)*

   a. God, please give me new and big opportunities.

   b. God, please help me prepare to be ready for opportunities when they come.

4. **In your opinion,** what does it mean to resolve to serve God and be a Christian? *(page 33)*

   _____

   _____

   _____

5. List three areas a man robs by refusing Christ. *(page 34)*

   a. _____

   b. _____

   _____

   c. _____

   _____

For Further Study

Seize the opportunity – Ephesians 5:15, 16; Examples: Rebekah in Genesis 24:55-67; David with Goliath in 1 Samuel 17; Shadrach, Meshach and Abednego in Daniel 3:8-30; Mary, the Lord's servant, in Luke 1:26-38; One criminal at the crucifixion in Luke 23:32-43.

Faithfulness is the cornerstone of character – *"A faithful man shall abound with blessings"* Proverbs 28:20; Matthew 24:45-47.

Decide to be a man of God, and write down your decision – *"But as for me and my house, we will serve the Lord"* Joshua 24:15. Decision motivates action – *"And Solomon determined to build an house for the name of the Lord"* 2 Chronicles 2:1. Write the decision so you'll be motivated to hold to it – *"Write the vision, and make it plain upon tables, that he may run that readeth it"* Habakkuk 2:2. Dedication and discipline enable you to overcome all obstacles – Isaiah 50:7; *"For Ezra had prepared his heart to seek the law of the Lord, and to do it, and to teach in Israel statues and judgments"* Ezra 7:10.

6. According to our text, how can a man become a counterfeit trinity? *(page 34)*

    _____

    _____

    _____

7. Where will men likely go after death if they do the following? *(pages 34-35)*

    a. Call God a liar and His Word meaningless   ____ Heaven   ____ Hell

    b. Take God's place in others' lives   ____ Heaven   ____ Hell

    c. Support Satan against God   ____ Heaven   ____ Hell

    d. Believe and confess that Jesus Christ is Lord   ____ Heaven   ____ Hell

---

For Further Study

Calling God a liar – *"If we say that we have not sinned, we make him a liar, and his word is not in us"* 1 John 1:10; *"He that saith, I know him, and keepeth not his commandments, is a liar, and the truth is not in him"* 1 John 2:4; *"Who is a liar but he that denieth that Jesus is the Christ? He is antichrist, that denieth the Father and the Son"* 1 John 2:22.

Confession – *"Whosoever therefore shall confess me before men, him will I confess also before my Father which is in heaven"* Matthew 10:32. *"Also I say unto you, Whosoever shall confess me before men, him shall the Son of man also confess before the angels of God"* Luke 12:8. *"That if thou shalt confess with thy mouth the Lord Jesus, and shalt believe in thine heart that God hath raised him from the dead, thou shalt be saved. For with the heart man believeth unto righteousness; and with the mouth confession is made unto salvation"* Romans 10:9-10.

Practical:

1. What are some belief systems that have caused you harm or difficulty? What belief systems do you see in others that you would like to emulate? _____
    _____

2. What are some areas of your life that you know are the result of wrong belief systems that have been in place for years?_____
    _____

3. What will you do to change these harmful belief systems? What is the first step for you?
    _____
    _____

4. What is the counterfeit trinity, and what has it done in your life? *(page 34)*
    _____
    _____

Repeat this prayer out loud:

Father, in Jesus' Name, I repent for my wrong belief systems. Please help me renew my mind with Your Word and become a man who is ready to serve You wholly and take opportunities You give me. Amen.

For Further Study

Making choices – *"I call heaven and earth to record this day against you, that I have set before you life and death, blessing and cursing: therefore choose life, that both thou and thy seed may live"* Deuteronomy 30:19; The freedom to choose between alternatives is the only true freedom in life – Galatians 5:13. As Christians, we can choose to succeed or fail; we can be wise or ignorant – Psalm 90:12. Our choices are shown by the company we keep – Proverbs 27:19 TLB. *"I will go"* Genesis 24:58. *"Choose you this day whom ye will serve"* Joshua 24:15. *"When Naomi realized that Ruth was determined"* Ruth 1:15-18 NIV. *"How long will you waiver between two opinions?"* 1 Kings 18:21 NIV. *"Be it known unto thee, O king, that we will not serve thy gods, nor worship the golden image which thou hast set up"* Daniel 3:18. *"I press toward the mark"* Philippians 3:12-21.
Renew your mind – Colossians 3:9-10; *"And be not conformed to this world: but be ye transformed by the renewing of your mind, that ye may prove what is that good, and acceptable, and perfect will of God"* Romans 12:2.

Self Test *Lesson 2*

1. Genesis 50:20 states *"What Satan meant for harm, God turned around for good."* Can our enemies take the good thing God has placed in us and try to use it against us? _____ Yes _____ No

2. What character trait will always outlast persecution? _____

3. A person's belief systems hold the greatest potential for _____ or _____ in life.

4. Is it possible for someone to "not believe anything"? _____ Yes _____ No

5. To believe in the positive, men must discipline themselves away from sin. _____ True _____ False

6. Belief is the basis for three things we studied. What are they?

   a. _____   b. _____   c. _____

7. Name five common characteristics of financially successful businessmen.

   a. _____   d. _____

   b. _____   e. _____

   c. _____

8. Which is more important? *(circle one)*
   a. to pray for opportunities to come   b. to pray to be ready for opportunities when they do come

9. Who is the counterfeit trinity?   a. _____   b. _____   c. _____

Keep this test for your own records.

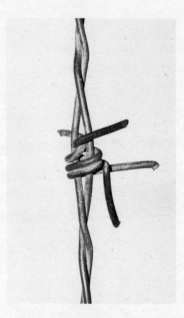

Lesson 3
My Brother's Keeper

Lesson 3
My Brother's Keeper

A.   Read Daniel 3.

  1.   A man's companions say much about his what? *(circle one)* *(page 39)*
       a. alma mater   b. life   c. character

  2.   Read: *"He that walketh with wise men shall be wise: but companion of fools shall be destroyed"* Proverbs 13:20.

  3.   Daniel had three friends who were of like precious faith. Who were they? *(page 39)*

       _____

B.   The Faith of a Friend

  1.   Read Acts 15. Why did Barnabas and Paul go their separate ways? _____

       _____

  2.   What must a man have to make it through tough times? *(circle all that apply)* *(page 43)*
       a. faith in others   b. cash reserves   c. faith in God's work

  3.   Read: *"Now faith is being sure of what we hope for and certain of what we do not see"* Hebrews 11:1 NIV.

For Further Study

Lay a right foundation for your character – 2 Corinthians 7:1. God commits to character, not talent – *"Well done, thou good and faithful servant: thou hast been faithful over a few things, I will make thee ruler over many things: enter thou into the joy of thy Lord"* Matthew 25:21; Luke 16:10; 2 Timothy 2:2.

When a man honors God, he strengthens his character, increases the stature of his manhood and finds favor with God and man – Job 17:9; Psalms 84:5, 7; 89:17; Proverbs 4:18; Daniel 1:6-7; Luke 2:40, 52. *"I have refrained my feet from every evil way, that I might keep thy word. I have not departed from thy judgments: for thou hast taught me … Through thy precepts I get understanding: therefore I hate every false way"* Psalm 119:101, 102, 104.

C.   The Substance Called Faith

1. Enthusiasm is an _____. Optimism is an _____. Faith is a _____.

2. Why is strengthening your faith now like buying insurance? *(page 44)*

    _____

3. Use words from the following list to fill in the blanks below: *(page 45)*

    failure   tests   success   prove

    God _____ us in order to _____ us. He sets us up for _____,

    not _____.

4. Read: *"He that observeth the wind shall not sow; and he that regardeth the clouds shall not reap"* Ecclesiastes 11:4. Rephrase the verse **in your own words.**

    _____

    _____

5. Hearing from God does not depend on age but on _____. You're

    never too _____ and never too _____. *(page 45)*

For Further Study

Faith in God honors Him; unbelief dishonors Him – *"Now the just shall live by faith … we are … of them that believe to the saving of the soul"* Hebrews 10:38, 39. *"But without faith it is impossible to please him: for he that cometh to God must believe that he is, and that he is a rewarder of them that diligently seek him"* Hebrews 11:6. Endurance – *"So that we ourselves glory in you in the churches of God for your patience and faith in all your persecutions and tribulations that ye endure"* 2 Thessalonians 1:4; *"Thou therefore endure hardness, as a good soldier of Jesus Christ"* 2 Timothy 2:3; *"And so, after he had patiently endured, he obtained the promise"* Hebrews 6:15; 11:27.
Men must be tested and proven before they can be given authority – James 1:12. One of the tests of manhood is how a man handles pressure – Proverbs 24:10.

6. Write out Hebrews 11:6. _____
    _____
    _____
    _____

7. Write out Hebrews 4:2. _____
    _____
    _____
    _____

D. The Greater Faith

1. Read: *"Yea, they turned back and tempted God, and limited the Holy One of Israel"* Psalm 78:41.

2. One of the most difficult things for many men to believe is that God believes in them! You must see the need to have faith in God, because God _____. *(page 47)*

3. When you limit yourself, you limit _____; when you limit _____, you limit _____. *(page 48)*

For Further Study

Trusting God and his transcendent glory – Proverbs 23:19; 1 Corinthians 1:9; Ephesians 1:11

Love and trust – *"For the king trusts in the Lord; through the unfailing love of the Most High he will not be shaken"* Psalm 21:7 NIV; *"He shall not be afraid of evil tidings: his heart is fixed, trusting in the Lord"* Psalm 112:7; *"Charge them that are rich in this world, that they be not high minded, nor trust in uncertain riches, but in the living God, who giveth us richly all things to enjoy"* 1 Timothy 6:17; 1 John 4:10.

Develop your own relationship with God – *"Even the Spirit of truth; whom the world cannot receive, because it seeth him not, neither knoweth him: but ye know him; for he dwelleth with you, and shall be in you"* John 14:17

You are never too young to hear from God. Hearing from God doesn't depend on age, but on relationship – *"My sheep hear my voice, and I know them: and they follow me"* John 10:27. Example: Samuel – 1 Samuel 3:4-10

4. Read: *"Now to Him Who, by (in consequence of) the [action of His] power that is at work within us, is able to [carry out His purpose and] do superabundantly, far over and above all that we [dare] ask or think [infinitely beyond our highest prayers, desires, thoughts, hopes, or dreams]—To Him be glory in the church and in Christ Jesus throughout all generations forever and ever. Amen (so be it)"* Ephesians 3:20-21 AMP.

Practical:

1. Do you have "close" friends—those you can confide in and be nakedly honest before? Have you made yourself truly accountable to another man who is spiritually much older than yourself? Who are some possible candidates?

   _____

2. How importantly do you view "risk" when it comes to being transparent with someone? What are the dangers? What are the benefits? Which outweigh the other? _____

   _____

   _____

   _____

Repeat this prayer out loud:

Father, I come before You, recognizing my tremendous need of You and my need of others as well. You placed me in the world to have relationships, and I choose relationships now by faith, even if it means moving out of my area of comfort. I thank You in advance for providing me with men in whom I can trust and with whom I can be myself. In Christ's Name, I pray. Amen.

For Further Study

Romans 16:25; 2 Corinthians 9:8; Ephesians 3:7; Hebrews 4:2

Self Test *Lesson 3*

1. What is one way of discovering a man's character? By observing who his _____ are

2. We spoke of three things that Daniel and his three friends had alike. They were:
   a. Each of them had an uncommon _____.
   b. Each of them held an uncommon _____.
   c. Each of them underwent an uncommon _____.

3. Why shouldn't the failure of one person whom we've trusted stop us from believing in another?
   _____
   _____

4. Paul and Barnabas had a dispute over another Bible character. Who was it? _____

5. Both Paul and Barnabas gave up on the third man above and knew he'd continue to be a failure.
   _____ True   _____ False

6. Match the words below to the correct description: a. enthusiasm   b. optimism   c. faith
   _____ an attitude   _____ a substance   _____ an emotion

7. According to Scripture, what is the outcome of "waiting for perfect conditions"? _____
   _____.

8. A young man must reach the age of accountability before he can hear from God.   _____ True   _____ False

9. God has no faith in mankind.   _____ True   _____ False

Keep this test for your own records.

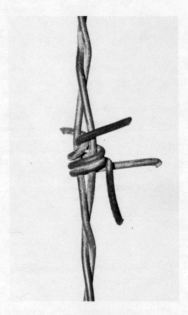

Lesson 4
Daring Discipline

Lesson 4
Daring Discipline

A. Read Daniel 4.

1. The United States is caught in a _____ that threatens the nation's heritage. **In your own words,** state what this means. *(page 49)*_____

_____

_____

2. "The character of our children is the _____ of our future as a culture ... when our children are _____, there is no higher priority than to seek their healing" Sen. Dan Coats. *(page 50)*

3. We are experiencing a rise of violence in our children. **In your own words,** what cultural trends have contributed to this? *(page 50)* _____

_____

4. Being nice is not always being loving. *(page 51)*   ____ True   ____ False

5. It is possible for others to be stronger in their rebellion than we are in our righteousness. *(page 51)*
____ True   ____ False

For Further Study

Fathers have a God-given responsibility to their offspring. Fathers are blessed when they raise their children in the fear and admonition of the Lord – Deuteronomy 11:18-21, but cursed if they neglect them – Proverbs 17:25.
Teach and train – *"Impress them on your children"* – Deuteronomy 6:5-9 NIV; *"Teach them to your children"* Deuteronomy 11:18-21 NIV; Ephesians 6:4; Colossians 3:16; 1 Thessalonians 4:1-8.
What to teach – 1 Timothy 4:11-13 NIV; Titus 2:2-8
Who should teach – Fathers and Mothers – Proverbs 1:8, 9; 4:1; 6:20-24; Elders – 1 Timothy 1:18; 4:14
Father's responsibilities for children – Ephesians 6:4; Colossians 3:21; 1 Timothy 3:4, 12
Abraham's example – *"He will direct his children and his household after him to keep the way of the Lord by doing what is right and just"* Genesis 18:19 NIV; Job 29:11-25; Proverbs 20:11; 22:6, 15; 23:13; 31:10-31.

6. God wants us to be single-minded about our convictions. Write out James 1:8.

_____

B. The Traits of True Love
1. Fill in the following with either "love" or "lust." *(page 51)*

_____ is not license.   _____ is the spirit of Heaven.

_____ has restraints.   _____ is the spirit of Hell.

_____ has no limits to doing evil.

2. Name the seven characteristics of love that accompany salvation. *(page 51)*

a. love of the _____   e. love of _____

b. love of the _____   f. love of the _____

c. love of the _____   g. love of _____

d. love of the _____

3. Our self-discipline as believers is born out of what? *(circle one)* *(page 52)*

a. our self image   b. our motivation for missions   c. our love for God

4. When we're self-disciplined, it's easy to what? *(circle one)* *(page 52)*

a. bring discipline into the home   b. lose weight   c. limit behavior

5. What do we mean by "love limits behavior"? *(page 52)* _____

_____

For Further Study

Definitions of Love – 1 Corinthians 13:4-8
Evidences of Love – *"Love is … never haughty or selfish or rude. Love does not demand its own way …
If you love someone … you will always believe in him, always expect the best of him, and always stand your
ground in defending him"* 1 Corinthians 13:4, 5, 7 TLB; John 17:23 NIV.
Love, not lust – Zephaniah 3:17; *"From whence come wars and fightings among you? come they not hence, even
of your lusts that war in your members?"* James 4:1, 2.
Lust is degenerative – 2 Samuel 13:1, 13-15; Proverbs 13:15; Isaiah 57:20, 21; James 1:14, 15.
Lust is insatiable, love is easily satisfied – Ecclesiastes 5:10; 1 Corinthians 13:4; James 4:1-3.

C.   The Blame Game

   1.   It is easier to blame others as the cause of negative consequences rather than _____

   _____. *(page 53)*

   2.   What are some of the consequences of guilt in a man's life? *(page 53)* _____

   _____

   _____

   3.   To eliminate guilt, what must be eliminated? *(circle one)* *(page 53)*

   a. religion   b. bad feelings   c. the cause

   4.   If Christianity becomes privatized, a "private matter," what else can happen? *(page 54)* _____

   _____

D.   Developing Discipline
   1.   Read: *"Better a patient man than a warrior, a man who controls his temper than one who takes a city"* Proverbs 16:32 NIV.

   2.   When did Daniel start developing discipline? *(page 56)* _____

   3.   In what areas did Daniel demonstrate his discipline? *(page 56)* _____

   4.   From Scripture, what do we see produced in Daniel as a result of fasting? *(pages 56-57)*

   _____

For Further Study

Lust limits, love releases – John 10:10; 15:13; Acts 20:35; Romans 12:9-10; 1 Corinthians 13:4-7; Ephesians 5:25; 2 Timothy 3:2; Hebrews 13:4; James 4:1-3; 1 Peter 4:8-10.

Love God's Word – *"O how love I thy law! it is my meditation all the day"* Psalm 119:97; Titus 2:7; James 1:21, 22.

Love centers in the will – *"I demand that you love each other as much as I love you"* John 15:12 TLB; *"Love the brotherhood. Fear God. Honour the king. Servants, be subject to your masters"* 1 Peter 2:17, 18.

The Holy Spirit is given to restrain – *"And I will put my spirit within you, and cause you to walk in my statutes, and ye shall keep my judgments, and do them"* Ezekiel 36:27; Deuteronomy 30:19.

Discipline is necessary – Proverbs 5:23; 22:6, 15; 23:13, 14 AMP; Hebrews 12:10, 11.

Keep your word to God – Deuteronomy 23:21; Poverbs 12:22; 13:24; 19:3 TLB; Matthew 21:28-31.

5. In what area does man's will reside? *(circle one)* *(page 57)*

    a. spirit   b. soul   c. body

6. In what area does man establish his purposes? *(circle one)* *(page 57)*

    a. mind   b. will   c. emotion

E. The Seventh Sense

1. Describe "seventh" sense as spoken of in our text. *(page 57)* _____

    _____

    _____

2. What has authority over the downward pull toward the earthy and human? *(circle one)* page 58)

    a. God   b. nothing can counteract it   c. spiritual strength

3. What causes a "downward pull" in our lives? *(page 59)* _____

4. Read Galatians 5:19-23.

5. Write out Galatians 4:9. _____

    _____

For Further Study

Maturity comes with the acceptance of responsibility – Genesis 3:11-12; Proverbs 16:2; 21:2; Acts 13:22.
Discipline must be done in love – Proverbs 13:24; Hebrews 12:5-7; *"Discipline your son while there is hope, but do not [indulge your angry resentments by undue chastisements and] set yourself to his ruin"* Proverbs 19:18 AMP.
Ideal – *"Don't let anyone think little of you because you are young. Be their ideal; let them follow the way you teach and live; be a pattern for them in your love, your faith, and your clean thoughts"* 1 Timothy 4:12 TLB.
Cleanse your spirit – *"Wherewithal shall a young man cleanse his way? by taking heed thereto according to thy word"* Psalm 119:9; John 15:3: 17:17 NIV.
Despite youth, you are a man – Jeremiah 1:6-8; You can hear from God – John 10:27; Watch unbridled passions – Proverbs 7:24, 25; 1 Corinthians 6:18.
Prayer – 2 Chronicles 15;2; Psalms 25:14; 51:6; 56:9; 73:25, 26; 145:18; Proverbs 3:32; Jeremiah 33:3; Luke 18:1; Acts 4:31; Romans 8:31, 37; Ephesians 6:18; Philippians 4:6; James 5:16, 17

F.   The Secret of Fasting

1.   You can fast from things other than food to cut off your attachment to earthy things. *(page 60)*
     ____ True   ____ False

2.   Fasting and devoting time to the Bible and prayer does what? *(circle all that apply) (page 60)*

     a. energizes your spirit   c. makes you lose weight

     b. brings your body and soul under subjection   d. increases the presence of God in your life

3.   When men find _____ and base their

     _____, they become

     successful in all they do. All the _____ and _____ of the

     Bible are the _____ to the Kingdom. *(page 61)*

G. Gaining Self-Discipline

1.   Man's will is able to do what four things? *(page 63)*

     a. _____   c. _____

     b. _____   d. _____

                                                     _____

For Further Study

Being led of the Spirit – *"For they that are after the flesh do mind the things of the flesh; but they that are after the Spirit the things of the Spirit"* Romans 8:5; Romans 8:9-11; *"For as many as are led by the Spirit of God, they are the sons of God"* Romans 8:14; *"And the spirit of the Lord shall rest upon him, the spirit of wisdom and understanding, the spirit of counsel and might, the spirit of knowledge and of the fear of the Lord"* Isaiah 11:2; See also Acts 2:17; 8:29; 10:19; 11:12; 1 Corinthians 2:11; 3:16.
Works of the flesh and works of the Spirit are found in Galatians 5:19-23.
Fasting – *"Then I proclaimed a fast there, at the river of Ahava, that we might afflict ourselves before our God, to seek of him a right way for us, and for our little ones, and for all our substance"* Ezra 8:21; Ezra 8:23; Daniel 9:3; See also Jesus' fast in the wilderness – Luke 4:1-14.
God's Word washes the mind and programs the conscience – Psalm 119:9; Ephesians 5:25-26; Colossians 3:16.

2. Name the two things the conscience allows us to do. *(page 63)*

    a. _____

    b. _____

3. Without _____ to the Word of God, behavior can be

    _____ to sanction any deed. *(page 63)*

4. We can trust the will of God, because God always _____ and _____
    toward our highest good. *(page 63)*

Practical:

1. What is meant by the proverb, *"Better to rule the spirit than take a city"* Proverbs 16:32?

    _____

    _____

2. Discuss with a friend if you can actually "will" to follow God.

Repeat this prayer out loud:

Father, I see the importance of disciplining myself and need Your help to do it. Help me to fast regularly, pray consistently and prepare myself for all that is coming ahead. I will to do Your will in Christ. Amen.

For Further Study

Learn from people, but seek your own pattern for living – *"Don't let the world around you squeeze you into its own mould, but let God re-make you"* Romans 12:2 Phillips.

God's Word gives the patterns and principles to overcome any obstacle, enemy or attack – *"Is not my word like as a fire? saith the Lord; and like a hammer that breaketh the rock in pieces?"* Jeremiah 23:29; *"For no word from God shall be void of power"* Luke 1:37 ASV; Numbers 23:19; Deuteronomy 29:29; Psalms 9:7-10; 90:1-2; 102:24-28; 136; Malachi 3:6-7; James 1:17.

What is submitted to grows stronger – Luke 4:4, 8, 12, 14; Romans 6:16; 12:2; Galatians 5:16; James 4:7.

God desires our highest good – Psalms 37:1-4; 84:11; Proverbs 23:18; Jeremiah 29:11; Romans 8:28.

Self Test *Lesson 4*

1. Being nice is not always being loving. _____ True _____ False

2. Love is not license. _____ True _____ False

3. Love has no restraints. _____ True _____ False

4. Name two of the seven characteristics of love that accompany salvation.

   a. love of _____ b. love of _____

5. The home is the _____ of the community. That's why failure to adhere to

   standards in the home will allow for failure in _____ life.

6. To eliminate guilt, what must be done? *(circle one)*

   a. blame someone else b. hold it in c. eliminate the cause

7. Give a short definition of what fasting does for the believer, as discussed in the text. _____

   _____

   _____

8. What are two things that our conscience allows us to do?

   a. _____ b. _____

9. We can always trust God's will because God always wills and works toward _____.

10. Prayerlessness is a form of _____.

Keep this test for your own records.

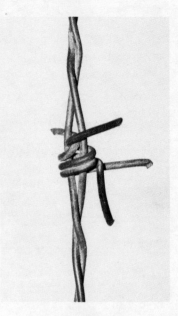

Lesson 5
Men Mature

Lesson 5
Men Mature

A. Read Daniel 7 *(note: This chapter chronologically follows Chapter 4).*

   1. How is maturity measured? *(circle one)* *(page 67)*

      a. age   b. level of social status achieved   c. acceptance of responsibility

   2. Every man since Adam has been charged with a three-fold responsibility, which is to: *(page 67)*

      a. _____   b. _____   c. _____

   3. Of all Daniel's knowledge, the greatest could not be acquired from his teachers in Israel nor the wise men of Babylon, _____. *(page 68)*

      That came from where? _____

   4. What is "God's good pleasure" for men? *(page 69)*

      _____

      _____

      _____

For Further Study

Maturity results from accepting responsibility – Acts 13:22.

We cannot mature if we blame circumstances and others – Proverbs 16:2; 21:2; See also Genesis 3:11-12.

We alone are responsible for our life – 2 Corinthians 5:10.

Every man is accountable for six areas of responsibility, based on 1 Timothy 3:1-11: Reputation – 1 Thessalonians 5:22; 2 Corinthians 6:3; Ethics – 1 Timothy 4:16; Morality and Temperament – 2 Timothy 2:24, 25; Habits – 1 Timothy 4:8; Maturity – 1 Timothy 4:15.

Daniel's favor and understanding – Daniel 1:8, 9, 17, 19

God's good pleasure – Ephesians 1:5-11; *"For it is God which worketh in you both to will and to do of his good pleasure"* Philippians 2:13; *"Wherefore also we pray always for you, that our God would count you worthy of this calling, and fulfil all the good pleasure of his goodness, and the work of faith with power"* 2 Thessalonians 1:11.

Crises can bring you closer to God – Romans 8:38.

B. Choosing Maturity

1. What must a man who is stale or cold in his Christian walk do? *(circle one)* *(page 70)*

    a. go back to his first love and develop a relationship with God through the Word and prayer

    b. get involved in church activities as many nights of the week as he is free

    c. let the season pass, waiting for a new one to start

2. Men who choose to mature, _____. *(page 71)*

C. Levels of Life

1. Life is lived on _____ and arrived at in _____. *(page 71)*

2. Every new level of responsibility, knowledge or authority calls for a further deepening of _____. *(page 71)*

3. Read: *"All the congregation of the Israelites moved on from the Wilderness of Sin by stages, according to the commandment of the Lord"* Exodus 17:1 AMP.

4. Read 2 Peter 1:5-7.

5. True maturity begins with _____ and culminates in _____, the full expression of _____. *(page 72)*

For Further Study

Build precept upon precept, from glory to glory – Psalm 119:173; Isaiah 28:10, 13; 2 Corinthians 3:18.

Character is built in private, out of a lifetime of decisions which enhance or diminish it – *"I have chosen the way of truth: thy judgments have I laid before me"* Psalm 119:30; *"If a man therefore purge himself from these, he shall be a vessel unto honour, sanctified, and meet for the master's use, and prepared unto every good work"* 2 Timothy 2:21.

When a man honors God, he strengthens his character, increases the stature of his manhood and finds favor with God and man – Job 17:9; Psalms 84:5, 7; 89:17; Proverbs 4:18; Luke 2:40, 52.

Maturation is a lifelong process – *"You, therefore, must be perfect [growing into complete maturity of godliness in mind and character, having reached the proper height of virtue and integrity], as your heavenly Father is perfect"* Matthew 5:48 AMP; Romans 5:3-5; 8:37; Galatians 6:9; Hebrews 3:6; 6:1; 1 John 3:2, 3.

6. What is meant by "The cross is either man's greatest blessing or his worst curse"? *(page 72)*

_____

_____

_____

_____

7. Those who want the crown in Heaven without accepting the cross while on earth are _____ of the cross. *(pages 72-73)*

8. Name the steps of destruction. *(page 73)*

Deception   D_____   D_____   Destruction

9. Modern church movements have unfortunately been marred in that they tended to omit the cross and ignore repentance. *(page 74)*   ____ True   ____ False

10. Success in life is not the _____ of the cross, but the _____ of it. *(page 74)*

11. No cross, no _____. *(page 74)*

D. Steps to Growth

1. Satan has the power to make us sin. *(page 75)*   ____ True   ____ False

2. Before we can deal ruthlessly with Satan, we must deal ruthlessly with _____. *(page 75)*

For Further Study

A man's word and character – Proverbs 21:8; 24:3, 4; Luke 6:45

Accept the cross – *"For the preaching of the cross is to them that perish foolishness; but unto us which are saved it is the power of God"* 1 Corinthians 1:18; 1 Corinthians 1:21, 23; 2:14; Colossians 2:14; Hebrews 12:2.

Pattern for failure – Deception: Genesis 3:4, 5; Distraction: Genesis 3:6; Dislocation: Genesis 3:7-10; Destruction: Genesis 3:23

Reward for overcoming – *"There is laid up for me a crown of righteousness"* 2 Timothy 4:8; *"Blessed is the man that endureth temptation: for when he is tried, he shall receive the crown of life, which the Lord hath promised to them that love him"* James 1:12; 1 Corinthians 10:13; 2 Corinthians 1:7; 1 Peter 4:13; Revelations 2:10.

3. Read James 4:7. What qualifies us to resist Satan? *(circle one)* *(page 75)*

    a. submission to God   b. confession of sin   c. fasting and prayer

4. What is submitted to grows _____. What is _____ grows weaker.

    True liberty is born out of _____. *(page 75)*

5. How do you get rid of the works of the flesh? *(circle all that apply)* *(page 75)*

    a. war against Satan   d. mortify (die to) the flesh

    b. experience Godly sorrow   e. reckon the devil dead

    c. have genuine repentance

6. Dying daily is the _____. *(page 76)* Read 1 Corinthians 15:30-34.

7. What is the only means of sin leaving a life? *(circle one)* *(page 76)*

    a. by way of the mouth   b. on your knees   c. in church

8. What did God say about "mixing seed" and what is the danger of it? *(pages 76-77)*

    _____

    _____

For Further Study

Repentance and resistance – *"Know ye not, that to whom ye yield yourselves servants to obey, his servants ye are to whom ye obey; whether of sin unto death, or of obedience unto righteousness?"* Romans 6:16; Psalm 34:14-16; 2 Corinthians 7:10; James 1:27; 1 John 1:9.

Crucify the flesh but live a resurrected life – *"For if we have been planted together in the likeness of his death, we shall be also in the likeness of his resurrection"* Romans 6:5; 2 Corinthians 7:1.

Flesh cannot produce what the Spirit produces – Isaiah 10:27; John 6:63; Romans 8:13; *"Mortify therefore your members which are upon the earth"* Colossians 3:5; 1 Corinthians 15:30-4.

Confess the Lord Jesus and confess your faults – Romans 10:9-10; James 5:16; 1 John 1:9.

Truth – *"And ye shall know the truth, and the truth shall make you free"* John 8:32; Isaiah 59:14; 2 Thessalonians 2:10; Base your life on truth – Proverbs 10:9; John 14:6; Not basing your life on truth – *"The way of transgressors is hard"* Proverbs 13:15; Truth is impartial – James 3:17.

9. What does the Word say about God's attitude toward things lukewarm? (Revelation 3:16) *(page 77)* _____

10. What sets you free? *(page 77)* ____ Sermons ____ Truth

11. Being right doesn't always make you _____. *(page 77)*

E. Gaining by Losing

1. There is no resurrection without _____, and no _____ without resurrection. *(page 77)*

2. Read James 4:10. What precedes blessing? *(page 78)* _____

3. All true joy is born out of _____. *(page 78)*

4. Read: *"A woman when she is in travail hath sorrow, because her hour is come: but as soon as she is delivered of the child, she remembereth no more the anguish, for joy that a man is born into the world"* John 16:21.

5. What is meant by "you gain by trading"? Define and give examples. *(page 78)* _____

_____

_____

For Further Study

Lukewarmness is mingled hot and cold – 2 Corinthians 6:14; Galatians 5:1; Revelations 3:15-16.
Truth brings freedom – *"And ye shall know the truth, and the truth shall make you free"* John 8:32; but it does not always bring popularity – John 7:6-7; 15:18, 19. Resurrection – *"That I may know him, and the power of his resurrection … If by any means I might attain unto the resurrection of the dead"* Philippians 3:10-11; Acts 4:2; Romans 1:4; 6:5; 1 Corinthians 15:42; 1 Peter 1:3. Humility – *"Humble yourselves [feeling very insignificant] in the presence of the Lord, and he will exalt you [He will lift you up and make your lives significant]"* James 4:10 AMP; 1 Proverbs 15:33; 18:12; 1 Peter 5:6. Joy from sorrow – Esther 9.22; *"Weeping may endure for a night, but joy cometh in the morning"* Psalms 30:5, 11; 126:5, 6; Jeremiah 31:9-17; John 16:20-21; 2 Corinthians 7:9.

6. What were the main areas where we see the "softness" of Israel? *(page 78)*

    a. _____   d. _____

    b. _____   e. _____

    c. _____   f. _____

Practical:

1. What is the difference between being "big-spirited" and "small-spirited"? *(pages 70-71)*

    _____

    _____

    _____

2. Look at the telltale signs of Israel growing "soft." Which of these most remind you of your own life? *(not necessary to write out) (page 78)*

3. Discuss with someone: What does it take to choose the way of the cross?

Repeat this prayer out loud:

Father, please forgive me for the areas of my life in which I've been lukewarm. I go to the cross now and ask for forgiveness, to have sin replaced with the righteousness and boldness of Jesus Christ. Help me to die to myself daily and return to the cross, so I can live my life on a whole new level. Amen.

For Further Study

Be ruthless with that for which Christ died – Romans 3:23-25; 2 Corinthians 5:21; Hebrews 2:17; 1 John 2:2; *"In this is love, not that we loved God, but that He loved us and sent His Son to be a propitiation for our sins"* 1 John 4:10 NASB.

Men who are soft – Joshua 18:3; *"Ye have not yet resisted unto blood, striving against sin"* Hebrews 12:4; Soft men cannot take rough times; they compromise with flesh – 1 Corinthians 10:13; Jesus was gentle but not soft – Mark 9:43, 44; 10:14; Soft men forfeit victory by seeking to avoid pain – 1 Corinthians 9:25.

Invest in character – *"Moreover it is required in stewards, that a man be found faithful"* 1 Corinthians 4:2; Proverbs 11:14; Matthew 7:15-16; *"You are not to keep company with anyone who claims to be a brother Christian but ... is greedy, or is a swindler ... Don't even eat lunch with such a person"* 1 Corinthians 5:11 TLB; Proverbs 29:2; 28:2; 2 Corinthians 7:1; 2 Peter 1:5-7.

Self Test *Lesson 5*

1. Maturity is measured by the acceptance of _____.

2. Man's three-fold responsibility since Adam is to:

   a. _____   b. _____   c. _____

3. Life is lived on _____ and arrived at in _____.

4. Each new level of revelation in a man's life produces the need for _____

   _____.

5. There is one line of demarcation between those who have been purged of their sins and those still in their

   sins. What is it? _____

6. Modern church movements have unfortunately been marred in that they tended to omit the cross and

   ignore repentance.   ____ True   ____ False

7. No cross, no _____.

8. Satan has the power to make us sin.   ____ True   ____ False

9. What do we mean by "die daily"? _____

   _____

   _____

10. God's intent is that sermons set you free.   ____ True   ____ False

Keep this test for your own records.

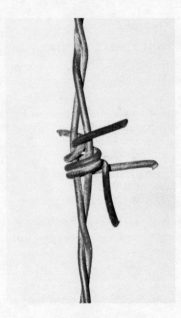

Lesson 6

The Great Rip-Off

Lesson 6
The Great Rip-Off

A. Read Daniel 8. To be conformed to the image of Christ, our _____ must be conformed to

_____. *(page 82)*

B. Five Propositions Concerning God's Word

1. Use the following word list to fill in the blanks of the sentences below: *(pages 82-84)*

character   source   name   absolute   nature   conduct   bond   faith

a. God's Word is His _____.

b. God's Word is the expression of His _____.

c. God's Word is the measure of His _____.

d. God's Word is magnified above His _____.

e. God's Word is the sole _____ of _____ and the _____

rule of _____.

2. What do we mean by God's Word "being His bond"? *(page 82)* _____

_____

3. Read: *"I will worship toward thy holy temple, and praise thy name for thy lovingkindness and for thy truth: for thou hast magnified thy word above all thy name"* Psalm 138:2.

For Further Study

To remain free from sin, program your conscience to righteousness by the Word of God – *"Let the word of Christ dwell in you richly in all wisdom"* Colossians 3:16.

God's Word is the source of truth – John 17:7; God's Spirit guides us into all truth – *"Howbeit when he, the Spirit of truth, is come, he will guide you into all truth"* John 16:13.

Words are powerful – *"Death and life are in the power of the tongue"* Proverbs 18:21.

God's Word – Luke 21:33; John 1:1; 14:9; *"For when God made promise to Abraham, because he could swear by no greater, he sware by himself"* Hebrews 6:13; *"And the Word was made flesh, and dwelt among us, (and we beheld his glory as of the only begotten of the Father,) full of grace and truth"* John 1:14; Revelations 1:8.

4. As creative power is in God's Word, so creative power is in man's word. Therefore, man speaks into existence _____ and _____ that have never existed before. *(page 86)*

5. Read: *"But I tell you, on the day of judgment men will have to give account for every idle (inoperative, nonworking) word they speak. For by your words you will be justified and acquitted, and by your words you will be condemned and sentenced"* Matthew 12:36-37 AMP.

C. Five Propositions Concerning Our Word

1. God watches over His Word to perform it (Jeremiah 1:12). How can we do this? *(page 87)*

   _____

   _____

   _____

2. Our word is our _____. *(page 87)*

3. Where men don't hold to a high value of truth, they don't place a high value on _____ _____. *(page 87)*

4. What do our words reveal about us? *(circle one)* *(page 88)*

   a. our nature   b. what movies we've seen   c. who we run around with

5. Integrity in our words is vitally important to God. Read: *"In whose eyes a vile person is condemned; but he honoureth them that fear the Lord. He that sweareth to his own hurt, and changeth not"* Psalm 15:4.

For Further Study

Creation story – Genesis 1; God created man with His characteristics – *"And God said, Let us make man in our image, after our likeness; and let them have dominion over the fish of the sea, and over the fowl of the air, and over the cattle, and over all the earth, and over every creeping thing that creepeth upon the earth"* Genesis 1:26.
God watches His Word – *"I am watching over My word to perform it"* Jeremiah 1:12 NASB.
Satan wants to destroy our word – Mark 4:15; John 10:10.
We must watch our word – Colossians 3:16; Titus 1:16; James 3:2; *"Wherefore putting away lying, speak every man truth with his neighbour: for we are members one of another"* Ephesians 4:25; *"Keep control of your tongue, and guard your lips from telling lies"* 1 Peter 3:10; 4:11 TLB.
Avoid false accusation – 2 Timothy 3:3; Revelations 12:10.

6. Explain "swearing to his own hurt"? *(page 89)* _____

    _____

7. Our name is only as good as _____. *(page 90)*

8. To whom is our word their rule of conduct? *(page 90)* _____

9. Read aloud John 10:10. What does Satan hope to gain by attacking God's Word? *(page 90)*

    _____

    _____

10. All sin pleases and serves. *(page 91)*   ____ True   ____ False

11. In Jesus' teaching of the parable of the sower (Mark 4:13-20), what will always happen when God's
    Word has been sown? *(page 91)* _____.

    What comes immediately after conversion? _____

    _____

12. What does a man teach his wife and children when he consistently makes promises he does not

    keep? *(page 92)* _____

13. Trust is always extended to the _____ and no more. *(page 92)*

For Further Study

"A good man out of the good treasure of his heart bringeth forth that which is good; and an evil man out of the evil treasure of his heart bringeth forth that which is evil: for of the abundance of the heart his mouth speaketh" Luke 6:45.
Our word – Psalm 24:3, 4; Proverbs 25:13, 19; Giving your word – Proverbs 6:1-5
Idle words – *"But I say unto you, That every idle word that men shall speak, they shall give account thereof in the day of judgment"* Matthew 12:36; *"The just man walketh in his integrity"* Proverbs 20:7.
Cleansed from idle words – *"Who can understand his errors? cleanse thou me from secret faults"* Psalm 19:12;
"Search me, O God, and know my heart: try me, and know my thoughts: And see if there be any wicked way in me, and lead me in the way everlasting" Psalm 139:23, 24; Psalm 25:5; Proverbs 26:2; Matthew 5:23-24; 1 John 1:9.

D.   Confronting Truth

Write out Ephesians 4:25. _____

_____

_____

Practical:

1.   Who do you know, that when you hear his name, past experience tells you his word can't be trusted, whether to be on time or to show up? What do others immediately think when they hear your name? *(no need to write out)*

2.   What has God spoken to you, in times past, that you've allowed Satan to steal?

_____

_____

3.   Read and discuss with a friend Matthew 12:36-37 and Ephesians 4:25.

Repeat this prayer out loud:

Father, in Jesus' Name, please forgive me for every time I have not been a man of my word. I want to reject other men's sins as well in which I may have been a partaker. I thank You that I can take You at Your Word. Help me, Father, to be a man of my word. Amen.

For Further Study

Hear and do the word – Mark 4:13-20.
Crisis in Truth – *"Know the truth"* John 8:32; *"The Spirit of truth … will guide you into all truth"* John 16:13; *"And judgment is turned away backward, and justice standeth afar off: for truth is fallen in the street, and equity cannot enter"* Isaiah 59:14; *"The lip of truth shall be established for ever: but a lying tongue is but for a moment"* Proverbs 12:19; Proverbs 12:22; Isaiah 59:15; 2 Timothy 3:12-13.
Every man must be grounded in truth – *"Sanctify them through thy truth: thy word is truth"* John 17:17; *"Seeing ye have purified your souls in obeying the truth through the Spirit"* 1 Peter 1:22; *"And it is the Spirit that beareth witness, because the Spirit is truth"* 1 John 5:6; *"Howbeit when he, the Spirit of truth, is come, he will guide you into all truth"* John 16:13.

Self Test *Lesson 6*

1. Conforming to the image of Christ requires our _____ conforming to God's Word.

2. God's Word is His _____.

3. When God entered into covenant agreement with Abraham, whom did He swear by? _____

4. God's Word is the expression of His _____ and the measure of His _____.

5. God's Word is magnified above His _____.

6. God's Word is the sole _____ of _____ and the absolute _____

    of _____.

7. In God's creative endowment to man in Genesis, He gave man creative power in his loins and _____.

8. Where men don't hold to a high value of truth, they don't place a high value on _____.

9. Our name is only as good as what? _____

10. What does Satan hope to gain by attacking God's Word? _____

    _____

11. In the parable of the sower, Jesus said Satan comes immediately to steal the word that was sown. How does

    a "word" get stolen? _____

    _____

    _____

Keep this test for your own records.

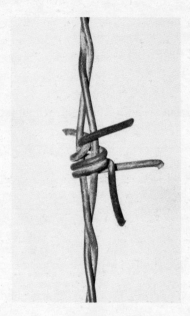

Lesson 7
The Greatest Gift

Lesson 7
The Greatest Gift

A. Read Daniel 5 *(note: This chapter chronologically follows Chapter 8).*

1. What kind of men did Daniel serve? *(page 98)*

   _____

2. Did Daniel need to forgive them? *(page 98)* ____ Yes ____ No

3. Through serving them, Daniel became qualified to _____. *(page 98)*

4. Forgiveness opens, unforgiveness _____. *(page 99)*

5. How are we to forgive? Write out Ephesians 4:32. _____

   _____

   _____

6. There is never a condition whereby God would not forgive us. *(page 99)* ____ True ____ False

7. When men experience tough times, the only way they can forgive is by the _____ of His _____. *(page 99)*

For Further Study

Daniel served men he had a right to hate – Daniel 1:1-6.

Forgiveness – Psalm 103:8-13; Micah 7:18-19; Romans 4:7, 8; *"Blessed is he whose transgressions are forgiven, whose sins are covered"* Psalm 32:1-7 NIV.

Forgiveness is in word and spirit – *"This is how my heavenly Father will treat each of you unless you forgive your brother from your heart"* Matthew 18:35 NIV; Psalm 49:7, 8; Mark 11:25-26; Ephesians 1:7; 2:8-9; 4:32.

The principle of release (John 20:21-23) states that only after sins are released are people free to become what God wants them to be – *"For if ye forgive men their trespasses, your heavenly Father will also forgive you: But if ye forgive not men their trespasses, neither will your Father forgive your trespasses"* Matthew 6:14-15; *"[Now having received the Holy Spirit, and being led and directed by Him] if you forgive the sins of anyone, they are forgiven; if you retain the sins of anyone, they are retained"* John 20:23 AMP.

8. Forgiveness is an expression of true: *(circle one)* *(page 99)*

   a. love   b. grace   c. holiness   d. mercy

B. Godly Forgiveness

   1. Forgiveness is always by _____. It is never _____. *(page 100)*

   2. The glory of God's type of forgiveness is that when He forgives, He remembers _____ _____ no more. *(page 101)*

   3. What happens when a man won't forgive, even when God has? *(page 101)*

      _____

      _____

C. Genuine Forgiveness

   1. When forgiveness is given, it must be offered in: *(circle one)* *(page 101)*

      a. sincere love.   b. a soft voice.   c. the same spirit in which it was asked.

   2. Forgiveness is always in spirit, not just in: *(circle one)* *(page 102)*

      a. attitude   b. action   c. word

   3. How did God give us evidence of His forgiveness? *(page 102)* _____

      _____

      _____

For Further Study

Healing takes place when, by faith, the principle of release is acted upon – Hebrews 12:1.

In order to activate this principle in your life, admit the Holy Spirit into your heart, and be guided and directed by Him – *"Then Jesus ... breathed on them, and said to them, Receive the Holy Spirit!"* John 20:21-22 AMP.

Grace – John 1:14-17; *"In whom we have redemption through his blood, the forgiveness of sins, according to the riches of his grace"* Ephesians 1:7; 2:5-8.

God forgives then forgets our sins – Psalms 32:1, 2; 85:2; 103:12; Isaiah 43:25; Romans 4:7, 8; *"O remember not against us former iniquities: let thy tender mercies speedily prevent us: for we are brought very low"* Psalm 79:8.

Develop a forgiving spirit – Romans 12:16; 1 Corinthians 1:10; Ephesians 4:3; Colossians 3:14.

4. What must we do to complete God's forgiveness? *(circle one)* *(page 103)*

a. ask for it   b. receive it   c. work for it

D. Extraordinary Forgiveness

1. Where the Holy Spirit ushers in forgiveness, what follows? *(circle one)* *(page 105)*

a. tears   b. love   c. release

2. If we're to be men of God, then we must understand that readiness to forgive must be an essential part of our character. By forgiveness, you do yourself a _____; by unforgiveness, a _____. *(page 107)*

3. Write out Mark 11:25-26. _____

_____

_____

_____

Practical:

1. God's Word tells us that if we don't forgive, He won't forgive. That sounds harsh! What are your thoughts as to why forgiveness is so important to God?

_____

_____

_____

For Further Study

The Holy Spirit – *"And grieve not the holy Spirit of God, whereby ye are sealed unto the day of redemption"* Ephesians 4:30; Ephesians 1:13; *"The Spirit itself beareth witness with our spirit, that we are the children of God"* Romans 8:16; *"Now we have received, not the spirit of the world, but the spirit which is of God; that we might know the things that are freely given to us of God"* 1 Corinthians 2:12; *"And because ye are sons, God hath sent forth the Spirit of his Son into your hearts, crying, Abba, Father"* Galatians 4:6; *"But as many as received him, to them gave he power to become the sons of God, even to them that believe on his name"* John 1:12.

2.   Who in your life has been the most difficult person to forgive? _____

How can you forgive him/her? _____

_____

_____

What is more important to you, holding on to the pain of a past hurt or obeying God through the power of His Spirit?

_____

3.   What steps can you take today to begin the process of reconciliation?

_____

_____

Repeat this prayer out loud:

Father, I realize that I cannot ask for Your forgiveness until I am first willing to forgive _____. So, as an act of obedience right now, I confess my forgiveness for him/her and ask You to help me forgive him/her daily until it becomes real in my life. Now, by faith, I ask You to forgive me of all my sins and cleanse me from all unrighteousness. I receive my forgiveness and thank You for Your faithfulness to me! Amen.

For Further Study

Giving the greatest gift – *"The words of the Lord Jesus, how he said, It is more blessed to give than to receive"* Acts 20:35; John 10:10, 11; 15:13; Romans 12:9, 10; 1 Corinthians 13:4-7; Ephesians 5:25; Hebrews 13:4; 1 Peter 4:8-10.

Self Test *Lesson 7*

1. What factor in Daniel's life was important to him becoming a leader?

    _____

2. We are to forgive: *(circle one)*

    a. when we feel able.   b. as Christ forgave us.   c. only if others say they are sorry.

3. Forgiveness _____. *(fill in the blank)*

    opens   closes   disappoints

4. We have the ability to forgive like God does in and of ourselves.   ____ True   ____ False

5. Forgiveness is always something that is earned.   ____ True   ____ False

6. Even though God will forgive us, He will still bring back to remembrance our sins in order to convict us.

    ____ True   ____ False

7. If we don't forgive, even when God has forgiven, we make ourselves:

    _____.

8. Forgiveness needs to be given in the same spirit in which it was asked.   ____ True   ____ False

9. It's one thing to pray for an answer but another thing to _____.

Keep this test for your own records.

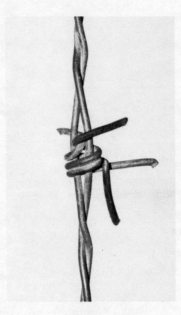

Lesson 8
Grit, Guts and Glory

Lesson 8
Grit, Guts and Glory

   A.   Read Daniel 9 *(note: This chapter chronologically follows Chapter 5).*

      1.   What is a definition of "sins of omission"? *(page 110)* _____

          _____

          _____

          _____

      2.   Write out James 4:17. _____

          _____

      3.   Lower morality leads to higher _____. *(fill in the blank)* *(page 110)*

          mortality   promiscuity   crime

      4.   Man was made a _____ creation, to live under a _____ government ruled

          by a _____ law and to be God's _____ agent on earth. *(page 111)*

For Further Study

Sin – *"Jesus said unto them, If ye were blind, ye should have no sin: but now ye say, We see; therefore your sin remaineth"* John 9:41; James 4:17; *"Because that, when they knew God, they glorified him not as God, neither were thankful; but became vain in their imaginations, and their foolish heart was darkened"* Romans 1:21; *"Thou that makest thy boast of the law, through breaking the law dishonourest thou God?"* Romans 2:23; *"All unrighteousness is sin: and there is a sin not unto death"* 1 John 5:17.

Morality toward others – *"The people of the land have used oppression, and exercised robbery, and have vexed the poor and needy: yea, they have oppressed the stranger wrongfully"* Ezekiel 22:29; Hosea 4:1-2; *"The good man is perished out of the earth: and there is none upright among men: they all lie in wait for blood; they hunt every man his brother with a net. That they may do evil with both hands earnestly, the prince asketh, and the judge asketh for a reward; and the great man, he uttereth his mischievous desire: so they wrap it up"* Micah 7:2-3; Romans 13:1-7.

B.   Morality Personified

1.   Who brought absolute morality into the world? *(page 111)* _____

2.   Read aloud Matthew 22:37-40.

3.   Everything that God revealed in the Old Testament, Jesus summed up in three sentences and two commandments. What were they? *(pages 111-112)* _____

_____

_____

_____

_____

4.   The substance of all true morality is the moral law of: *(circle one)* *(page 112)*

     a. love   b. Heaven   c. justification

5.   Loving what is immoral while professing to be moral agents of God is _____

_____. *(page 112)*

For Further Study

Absolute morality – *"And thou shalt love the Lord thy God with all thine heart, and with all thy soul, and with all thy might"* Deuteronomy 6:5; *"Jesus said unto him, Thou shalt love the Lord thy God with all thy heart, and with all thy soul, and with all thy mind. This is the first and great commandment. And the second is like unto it, Thou shalt love thy neighbour as thyself. On these two commandments hang all the law and the prophets"* Matthew 22:37-40; *"And he answering said, Thou shalt love the Lord thy God with all thy heart, and with all thy soul, and with all thy strength, and with all thy mind; and thy neighbour as thyself"* Luke 10:27.
Loving God over the world – *"Ye adulterers and adulteresses, know ye not that the friendship of the world is enmity with God? whosoever therefore will be a friend of the world is the enemy of God"* James 4:4; *"Love not the world, neither the things that are in the world. If any man love the world, the love of the Father is not in him. For all that is in the world, the lust of the flesh, and the lust of the eyes, and the pride of life, is not of the Father, but is of the world. And the world passeth away, and the lust thereof: but he that doeth the will of God abideth for ever"* 1 John 2:15-17.

C. The Contradiction of Modern Morals

1. What is today's media viciously manipulated by? *(page 113)*

   _____

2. What does the Bible plainly say regarding sexual immorality among Christians? *(page 113)*

   _____

3. Moral correspondence is the _____ God knows. *(page 115)*

4. Can a man love God with his lips but without his heart in agreement? *(page 115)*

   ____ Yes   ____ No

5. Men need to be moral in what areas? *(page 115)*

   _____

D. Thought – Father to the Deed

1. No man becomes immoral in deed without first becoming immoral in: *(circle one)* *(page 115)*

   a. habits   b. thought   c. his home

2. There is no seduction without _____. *(fill in the blank)* *(page 115)*

   sin   flirtation   revealing clothes

For Further Study

Scripture talks of "modern morality" – *"But fornication, and all uncleanness, or covetousness, let it not be once named among you … Neither filthiness, nor foolish talking, nor jesting, which are not convenient … For this ye know, that no whoremonger, nor unclean person, nor covetous man, who is an idolater, hath any inheritance in the kingdom of Christ and of God"* Ephesians 5:3-5; *"Now the works of the flesh are manifest, which are these; Adultery, fornication, uncleanness, lasciviousness, Idolatry, witchcraft, hatred, variance, emulations, wrath, strife, seditions, heresies, Envyings, murders, drunkenness, revellings, and such like"* Galatians 5:19-21.

Thought and motive – Matthew 15:8; Mark 7:6; *"Wherefore the Lord said, Forasmuch as this people draw near me with their mouth, and with their lips do honour me, but have removed their heart far from me, and their fear toward me is taught by the precept of men"* Isaiah 29:13; *"But every man is tempted, when he is drawn away of his own lust, and enticed. Then when lust hath conceived, it bringeth forth sin: and sin, when it is finished, bringeth forth death"* James 1:14-15; Genesis 50:20; Proverbs 15:26; Isaiah 59:7.

3.   What did King Balak do to seduce Balaam? What was Balaam seduced to do? *(page 115)*

_____

_____

4.   What happened as a result of Balaam's immorality? *(page 116)*

_____

5.   Write the correct letter from the right to define the following terms: *(page 116)*

_____ intellect   a. decides the issue

_____ sensibility   b. appeals to right or wrong

_____ will   c. discerns between right and wrong

6.   Reading the Bible: *(circle all that apply)* *(page 116)*

a. gives knowledge to the intellect.   c. inscribes God's commandments upon the heart.

b. programs the conscience.   d. fails to change a man.

7.   Read 1 Timothy 4:2.

8.   Someone with a "defiled" or "seared" conscience is still sensitive to morality. *(page 116)*

____ True   ____ False

9.   The conscience can be seared and then totally destroyed. *(page 116)*   ____ True   ____ False

For Further Study

"Flirtation" with Balaam – Numbers 22:7-11; 24:25; 25:1-5; *"And, behold, one of the children of Israel came and brought unto his brethren a Midianitish woman in the sight of Moses, and in the sight of all the congregation of the children of Israel, who were weeping before the door of the tabernacle of the congregation. And when Phinehas, the son of Eleazar, the son of Aaron the priest, saw it, he rose up from among the congregation, and took a javelin in his hand; And he went after the man of Israel into the tent, and thrust both of them through, the man of Israel, and the woman through her belly. So the plague was stayed from the children of Israel"* Numbers 25:6-9.

Programming the conscience – God's Word washes the mind and programs the conscience to righteousness. *"Christ also loved the church, and gave himself for it; That he might sanctify and cleanse it with the washing of water by the word"* Ephesians 5:25-26; Psalm 119:9.

E. The Ethics of Morality

1. To receive the Spirit of God and use it only to _____
    is immoral. *(page 117)*

2. What was the core of the temptation that Jesus faced when Satan tempted Him to turn stone
    into bread? *(page 117)*

    _____

    _____

    _____

3. Immorality can be in more areas than just sex. What are some other areas where issues can be
    seen as immoral? *(page 119)*

    _____

    _____

    _____

For Further Study

To remain free from sin, program your conscience to righteousness by the Word of God – *"Let the word of Christ dwell in you richly in all wisdom"* Colossians 3:16; *"All scripture is given by inspiration of God, and is profitable for doctrine, for reproof, for correction, for instruction in righteousness"* 2 Timothy 3:16.

Seared conscience – *"Speaking lies in hypocrisy; having their conscience seared with a hot iron"* 1 Timothy 4:2; *"And even as they did not like to retain God in their knowledge, God gave them over to a reprobate mind, to do those things which are not convenient"* Romans 1:28; *"Now as Jannes and Jambres withstood Moses, so do these also resist the truth: men of corrupt minds, reprobate concerning the faith"* 2 Timothy 3:8; *"They profess that they know God; but in works they deny him, being abominable, and disobedient, and unto every good work reprobate"* Titus 1:16.

Spirit of God – *"But ye shall receive power, after that the Holy Ghost is come upon you"* Acts 1:8.

Temptation of bread – Matthew 4:3-4; Luke 4:3-4

4. It may be tough to live morally, and tougher to stand up to immorality, but toughest of all is to live _____. *(page 119)*

Practical:

1. What do you think were Daniel's standards in politics? In personal finances? In listening to others? In choosing friends? In working for his boss? What things may have been in his thoughts that are not in your thoughts?

    _____

    _____

    _____

    _____

Repeat this prayer out loud:

Father, in Jesus' Name, please forgive me for every immoral thought or deed I've had. I desire to purify my thoughts, through the reading of Your Word. Help me, remind me, to do it daily. And I thank You for it. Amen.

For Further Study

Immorality in life – *"This I say then, Walk in the Spirit, and ye shall not fulfill the lust of the flesh. For the flesh lusteth against the Spirit, and the Spirit against the flesh: and these are contrary the one to the other: so that ye cannot do the things that ye would"* Galatians 5:16-17; Galatians 5:19, 24; 1 Corinthians 3:3; *"Mortify therefore your members which are upon the earth; fornication, uncleanness, inordinate affection, evil concupiscence, and covetousness, which is idolatry"* Colossians 3:5.

Moral wisdom – *"Who is a wise man and endued with knowledge among you? let him show out of a good conversation his works with meekness of wisdom. But if ye have bitter envying and strife in your hearts, glory not, and lie not against the truth. This wisdom descendeth not from above, but is earthly, sensual, devilish"* James 3:13-15.

Honoring heroes – *"I want the company of the godly men and women in the land; they are the true nobility"* Psalm 16:3 TLB; *"I will make the godly of the land my heroes, and invite them to my home. Only those who are truly good shall be my servants"* Psalm 101:6 TLB.

Self Test *Lesson 8*

1. What are "sins of omission"? _____

2. Lower morality leads to higher _____. *(fill in the blank)*

    mortality   promiscuity   crime

3. Who brought absolute morality into the world? _____

4. What moral law is the substance of all true morality? Two commandments: _____

    _____

    _____

    _____

    _____

5. God said a person who chose to be a "friend to the world" was _____.

6. Loving what is immoral while professing to be moral agents of God is _____.

7. No man becomes immoral in deed without first becoming immoral in _____.

8. There is seduction without flirtation.   ____ True   ____ False

9. Define a "seared conscience." _____

10. Which is more important: to practice what we preach or to preach what we practice? Why? _____

    _____

Keep this test for your own records.

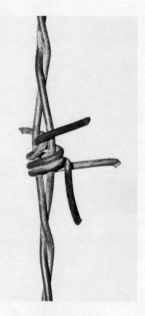

Lesson 9
Scriptural Illiteracy

Lesson 9
Scriptural Illiteracy

A. Read Daniel 6 *(note: This chapter chronologically follows Chapter 9).*

1. Our faith must be built upon a solid foundation of the Word. Read Matthew 7:24-27.

2. Which of the following are the foundational "bedrocks" on which to build a Christian life? *(circle all that apply)* *(pages 121-122)*

    a. what people say

    b. good advice

    c. reading the Bible

    d. reading articles

    e. praying

    f. listening to Christian radio

    g. fasting

    h. Christian television

    i. human wisdom

3. Counselors determine the _____ of kings. *(page 122)*

4. Good advice is based on _____. Godly counsel is based
    on the _____. *(page 122)*

For Further Study

Foundation – Matthew 7:24-27

Fasting – Ezra 8:21-22; Esther 4:16, 9:31; Jeremiah 36:6, 9; Daniel 9:3; Matthew 6:16-18

Prayer requires honesty with God – Psalm 51:6; *"The Lord is nigh unto all them that call upon him … in truth"* Psalm 145:18. True prayer is sharing with God the cares and needs of our lives and letting Him share with us His concern for the world – Philippians 4:6; *"Call unto me, and I will answer thee, and show thee great and mighty things, which thou knowest not"* Jeremiah 33:3. It is normal to pray – Luke 18:1; Ephesians 6:18. Neglect of prayer will separate us from God as much as yielding to temptation – 2 Chronicles 15:2.

Prayer leads to friendship with God – Friendship with God is life's greatest treasure – Psalm 25:14; Proverbs 3:32. Being with God dispels loneliness – Psalm 73:25, 26. Prayer leads to power with God. Men who know how to pray develop a boldness toward life that enables them to be more than conquerors – Romans 8:31, 37; James 5:16, 17. Those who know how to pray know that God is for them – Psalm 56:9. The result of prayer in private is boldness in public – *"And when they had prayed … they spake the word of God with boldness"* Acts 4:31.

5.   Name the three preliminaries to understanding a passage from the Bible. *(page 122)*

a. _____

b. _____

_____

c. _____

_____

6.   What happens to the man without an organized system of thought? *(page 122)* _____

_____

7.   Read Luke 10:27. This scripture claims we must love the Lord with our: *(circle one)* *(page 123)*

a. talent   b. works   c. mind

B.   Search for Truth

1.   Read Proverbs 2:4. According to this verse, when does truth come? *(page 124)*

_____

2.   _____ is a characteristic of real manhood. *(page 124)*

For Further Study

The Lord speaks to His children through prayer and through His Word – Luke 24:32. When David encountered his greatest crisis, he was able to strengthen himself by reviewing what God had done for him and His people in times past – 1 Samuel 30:6. To succeed in life, you must pay careful attention to God's Word. Write down what God tells you – Proverbs 7:2, 3. Study every word God gives you – Job 23:12.

Counselors determine the destiny of kings – 2 Samuel 16:23; 1 Kings 14.

As disciples, it is our right to know the truth – John 8:31, 32. Learn to discern between good and evil, the truth and a lie – 1 Kings 3:9. Don't be moved by every person's personality, persuasion and belief – Ephesians 4:14. *"Stop listening to teaching that contradicts what you know is right"* Proverbs 19:27 TLB; *"Only a simpleton believes what he is told! A prudent man checks to see where he is going"* Proverbs 14:15 TLB; *"And let the peace ... from Christ rule (act as umpire continually) in your hearts"* Colossians 3:15 AMP; *"But you have received the Holy Spirit and he lives within you, in your hearts ... he teaches you all things, and he is the Truth"* 1 John 2:27 TLB.

3.   Faith in our brothers is another characteristic of real manhood. *(page 126)*

____ True   ____ False

4.   Everyone who claims to be our "brother" probably is. *(page 126)*   ____ True   ____ False

5.   Write out 2 Timothy 2:15. _____

_____

_____

C.   The Lions in Our Lives

1.   What, symbolically, are "lions" in our lives? *(page 127)* _____

_____

_____

2.   What, symbolically, is a "lions' den" in our lives? *(page 127)* _____

_____

_____

For Further Study

Truth – Know the truth so you can recognize the lies of Satan and fight for the honor of God – Proverbs 2:6-9. The more you base your life on truth, the better will be your way and the greater will be your life – Proverbs 10:9; John 14:6. The more you base your life on a lie, the harder will be your way and the less significant will be your life – Proverbs 2:22, 13:15. Truth is eternal – Proverbs 12:19. Truth eliminates guilt, fear and secrecy and brings freedom – John 8:32. Men may know the truth, recognize truth and even admit to truth, yet still fall for deception if they do not love truth – 2 Thessalonians 2:10; *"Let everything you do reflect your love of the truth and the fact that you are in dead earnest about it"* Titus 2:7.

Obedience brings blessing – Deuteronomy 11:26-28; *"Cursed be the man that obeyeth not the words of this covenant"* Jeremiah 11:3.

Clothe yourself with Christ's humility – Deuteronomy 8:2-3, 16; 2 Chronicles 7:14; Proverbs 15:33; Philippians 2:1-11; James 4:10; 1 Peter 5:5-6.

Naaman and Elisha – 2 Kings 5

3.   Obedience to God's Word is all-important if we desire to see His blessing. Remember that

_____ precedes blessing. *(page 129)*

4.   **In your own words,** what was the major lesson that Naaman learned from his encounter with

Elisha? *(page 129)* _____

_____

D.   Wisdom Begets Strategy

1.   God's strategies are the product of His _____. *(page 129)*

2.   Write out Proverbs 4:7-8.

_____

_____

3.   He who has the wisdom of God has power over _____. *(page 129)*

For Further Study

Wisdom – James 1:5; 3:13-17; *"Wisdom is the principal thing; therefore get wisdom: and with all thy getting get understanding. Exalt her, and she shall promote thee: she shall bring thee to honour, when thou dost embrace her"* Proverbs 4:7-8.

God gives wisdom for strategy – Proverbs 3:19; *"Blessed be the Lord my strength, which teacheth my hands to war, and my fingers to fight"* Psalm 144:1; *"Wisdom strengtheneth the wise more than ten mighty men which are in the city"* Ecclesiastes 7:19; Psalms 17:4; 44:5; 2 Corinthians 2:14. Becoming wise – Proverbs 8:5; 13:16; *"If thou seekest her as silver, and searchest for her as for hid treasure"* Proverbs 2:4.

Agreement – *"If a kingdom be divided against itself, that kingdom cannot stand"* Mark 3:24; Mark 3:25-26; *"Two are better than one; because they have a good reward for their labour ... And if one prevail against him, two shall withstand him; and a threefold cord is not quickly broken"* Ecclesiastes 4:9-12.

Bramble bush – Judges 9:7-15

E. Boldness – An Achiever's Strategy

1. Summarize **in your own words** what we learn from the parable of the Bramble Bush.
    (pages 130-131) _____

    _____

2. What happens when good men abandon moral responsibility in the community? *(page 131)*

    _____

    _____

3. Weakness ascends when _____. *(page 132)*

4. Why must men be scripturally literate? *(page 132)* _____

    _____

5. Wisdom produces a _____ that leads to _____,

    resulting in _____. *(page 132)*

For Further Study

Victory requires a fight – 1 Corinthians 9:25-26; Colossians 1:29.

Victory from strategy brings glory – *"Thine, O Lord, is the greatness, and the power, and the glory, and the victory, and the majesty"* 1 Chronicles 29:11; 2 Chronicles 20:12; *"Be not afraid nor dismayed by reason of this great multitude; for the battle is not yours, but God's … set yourselves, stand ye still, and see the salvation of the Lord with you … fear not, nor be dismayed … for the Lord will be with you"* 2 Chronicles 20:15-17.

Be ready to answer – *"Let your speech be always with grace, seasoned with salt, that ye may know how ye ought to answer every man"* Colossians 4:6; 1 Peter 3:15.

Moral cowardice causes men to shrink from duty and danger, to dread pain and to yield to fear – Numbers 13:33; 1 Samuel 15:24. The fear of man is a form of moral cowardice – Proverbs 29:25.

Moral courage enables a person to encounter hatred, disapproval and contempt without departing from what is right – Psalm 119:157. Examples: Gideon – Judges 6, 7; David – 1 Samuel 17; Daniel – Daniel 6; John the Baptist – Matthew 14:3-10; Stephen – Acts 7; Paul – Acts 27; 28:1-5.

Practical:

1. Read Proverbs 1:7; 3:16-17; 4:7; 8:13; 9:10. What will wisdom such as this do for you?

   _____

   _____

2. With the rise of teen violence, what do you have to offer the next generation regarding the statement "It is better to have something worth dying for than to have nothing worth living for"?

   _____

   _____

Repeat this prayer out loud:

Father God, I will not follow a bramble bush, neither will I live as one. Please forgive me where I've been lax in my study of Your Word and have abdicated to the worldly and proud instead of being bold in my witness and lifestyle. Please give me wisdom to overcome my own laziness and a strategy to become a truly mighty man of God for the sake of Your Name and Your honor. In Christ's Name, I pray. Amen.

For Further Study

"Study to show thyself approved unto God, a workman that needeth not to be ashamed, rightly dividing the word of truth" 2 Timothy 2:15.

Who is a "brother"? – *"Not every one that saith unto me, Lord, Lord, shall enter into the kingdom of heaven: but he that doeth the will of my Father which is in heaven"* Matthew 7:21; Matthew 25:41-45.

"When there is moral rot within a nation, its government topples easily" Proverbs 28:2 TLB.

"Wisdom is the principal thing; therefore get wisdom: and with all thy getting get understanding" Proverbs 4:7;

"The fear of the Lord is the beginning of knowledge: but fools despise wisdom and instruction" Proverbs 1:7;

"The fear of the Lord is to hate evil: pride, and arrogancy, and the evil way, and the froward mouth, do I hate" Proverbs 8:13; *"The fear of the Lord is the beginning of wisdom: and the knowledge of the holy is understanding"* Proverbs 9:10; *"Length of days is in her right hand; and in her left hand riches and honour. Her ways are ways of pleasantness, and all her paths are peace"* Proverbs 3:16-17.

Self Test *Lesson 9*

1. Circle the foundational "bedrocks" on which to build a Christian life.

   a. what people say   d. good advice   g. reading the Bible

   b. reading articles   e. praying   h. Christian radio

   c. fasting   f. Christian television   i. human wisdom

2. Counselors determine the _____ of kings.

3. Good advice is based on _____.

   Godly counsel is based on the _____.

4. Three preliminaries to understanding a Bible passage are:

   a. Understand it _____.

   b. Understand it _____.

   c. Understand it _____

   _____.

5. Why is an organized system of thought so important for us? _____

   _____

6. Luke 10:27 claims we must love the Lord with our: *(circle one)*

   a. talent   b. works   c. mind

7. Everyone who claims to be our "brother" probably is.   ____ True   ____ False

8. What, symbolically, would be "lions" and "lions' dens" for us? _____

   _____

   _____

9. Weakness ascends when _____.

Keep this test for your own records.

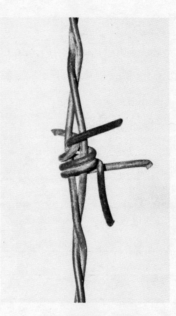

Lesson 10
The Power of a Four-Letter Word

Lesson 10
The Power of a Four-Letter Word

A. Read Daniel 10 *(note: This chapter chronologically follows Chapter 6).*

   1. Read aloud James 4:3. Give your own definition of "prayer abuse." *(page 133)*

   _____

   _____

   2. Prayer is like money and sex. *(page 133)* They were made for _____ and

   _____, not for _____ and _____.

   3. Read: *"Friendship with God is reserved for those who reverence him. With them alone he shares the secrets of his promises"* Psalm 25:14 TLB.

   4. Prayer is important to time management. *(page 133)*   ____ True   ____ False

   5. How can we add hours to our days? *(page 133)* _____

For Further Study

Prayer abuse – *"Ye ask, and receive not, because ye ask amiss, that ye may consume it upon your lusts"* James 4:3; *"The secret of the Lord is with them that fear him; and he will show them his covenant"* Psalm 25:14.
Love, not lust, satisfies – Zephaniah 3:17; John 10:10; 15:12, 13; 1 Corinthians 13:5; Ephesians 5:25; 2 Timothy 3:2; Hebrews 13:4; James 4:1-3.
Determine to follow after success and godliness – Deuteronomy 8:18.
Purify your motives and use your ego to achieve great things for God – Mark 12:30.
Concentrate on your strengths, not your weaknesses – Romans 12:6.
The power to resist is the key to success. Jesus Christ overcame temptation through the Word of God – Luke 4:4, 8, 12. His submission to the Father, resistance to the devil and refusal to sin strengthened His Spirit – Luke 4:14; To succeed in life as Jesus did, we must influence people to conform to our godly standard of behavior – Romans 12:2.

6. The secret to life's success is: *(page 134)*

    a. _____   c. _____

    b. _____   d. _____

7. Meditation is the _____ of _____. *(page 134)*

8. Explain the idea of "time abuse." *(page 134)* _____

    _____

    _____

B. Five Basic New Testament Prayers

    1. The Sinner's Prayer – A true sinner's prayer is marked by _____

        that begets _____ and leads to _____. *(page 135)*

For Further Study

Detail the will and plan of God for your life. Be a steward of God's words. Don't despise them by neglecting them – Isaiah 34:16; 1 Timothy 4:14-16. Write down everything he tells you – Deuteronomy 6:6, 9. Write down what God has taught you today and what He teaches you day by day in the future – Revelations 1:19. Details make the difference between success and failure – *"As the Lord commanded Moses his servant, so did Moses command Joshua, and so did Joshua; he left nothing undone of all that the Lord commanded Moses. So Joshua took all that land"* Joshua 11:15, 16. God is concerned with detail – Psalm 139:13, 14; Matthew 10:29, 30. The first step in attending to details is to write them down – Deuteronomy 17:18, 19. Discipline yourself to do what God tells you to do. Give God your immediate obedience – Psalm 119:60. Remember that an ounce of obedience is worth a ton of prayer – 1 Samuel 15:22; Psalm 40:6.

The Lord has plans for you – Jeremiah 29:11.

Man is not God – *"Many are the plans in a man's heart, but it is the Lord's purpose that prevails"* Proverbs 19:21 NIV; Psalm 33:11; Proverbs 16:9; 20:24.

THE POWER OF A FOUR-LETTER WORD

2. The Disciples' Prayer – The prayer Jesus taught His disciples is the prayer which is found in Luke 11:1-4. This prayer is a _____ in prayer that embraces the totality of a _____ and _____ on earth. *(page 135)*

3. The Lord's Prayer

   a. Where did this prayer take place? *(page 135)* _____

   b. What kind of prayer is it? *(page 135)*

   _____

   c. _____ to the will of God does not guarantee there will be no death, but that after death, there will be a _____. *(page 135)*

4. The Intercessor's Prayer – Intercession is always on behalf of another. _____, _____ for the _____ of the loved one and _____ for _____ are the evidences of God's love. *(page 136)*

5. The Devil's Prayer – What, in essence, is "The Devil's Prayer"? *(page 136)*

   _____

For Further Study

Crisis is normal to life – John 16:33. Crisis has sorrow in it, but sorrow is life's greatest teacher – Psalm 119:71; Ecclesiastes 7:3; 2 Corinthians 7:10. All true joy is born out of sorrow – Psalms 30:5; 126:5. God wants every change in the lives of His children to be good – Romans 8:28.
The Sinner's Prayer – Luke 18:13
The Disciples' Prayer – Luke 11:1-4
The Lord's Prayer – Luke 22:41-44
The Intercessor's Prayer – John 17:9-26
The Devil's Prayer – Mark 1:23-24

C.   The Benchmark of Prayer

1.   Strength in prayer gives _____ to character. *(page 138)*

2.   Prayer produces _____. *(page 138)*

3.   You become intimate with the one ... *(page 138)*

_____ whom you pray, _____ whom you pray and _____ whom you pray.

4.   Private prayer brings _____ in public appearances. *(page 138)*

5.   Write out Proverbs 28:1. _____

_____

_____

6.   Why do women typically pray more easily than men? *(page 139)*

_____

_____

_____

For Further Study

Prayer produces intimacy – *"They joined with the other believers in regular attendance at ... prayer meetings ... And all the believers ... shared everything with each other"* Acts 2:42-44 TLB.

Boldness is a form of courage – Proverbs 10:10 AMP, TLB; Hebrews 13:6; 1 Peter 3:15. Successful men are bold in their identification with their belief, product or activity and in their confession of it – Psalm 119:46; Romans 1:16; *"The wicked flee when no man pursueth but the righteous are bold as a lion"* Proverbs 28:1.

Overcome fear of man, openly identify with Jesus and be bold in confessing Him – *"And fear not them which kill the body, but are not able to kill the soul: but rather fear him which is able to destroy both soul and body in hell ... Whosoever therefore shall confess me before men, him will I confess also before my Father which is in heaven"* Matthew 10:28, 32, 33. *"And they overcame him (the devil) by the blood of the Lamb, and by the word of their testimony"* Revelations 12:11.

7. In your opinion, does this excuse men from learning to pray? _____ Yes _____ No

8. The Word of God is a _____, faith is a _____, and _____ is a _____. They all _____ you. *(page 139)*

9. Why doesn't prayer come naturally? *(page 139)* _____

_____

_____

D. Spiritual Muscle

1. Alcohol and drugs are an escape to bondage, while prayer is an _____ to _____. *(page 140)*

2. Trying to be "good" in the presence of God is a _____ and _____ effort. *(page 140)*

3. You don't get good then get to God, you get God, and He _____! *(page 140)*

4. The absence of prayer is testimony to _____ ability; the presence of prayer is testimony to _____ ability. *(page 141)*

For Further Study

What grace has provided, faith must obtain – *"Now faith is the substance of things hoped for, the evidence of things not seen"* Hebrews 11:1.

Don't try to "be good" in prayer – *"Two men went up into the temple to pray; the one a Pharisee, and the other a publican. The Pharisee stood and prayed thus with himself, God, I thank thee, that I am not as other man are … And the publican, standing afar off, would not lift up so much as his eyes unto heaven, but smote upon his breast, saying, God be merciful to me a sinner. I tell you, this man went down to his house justified rather than the other: for every one that exalteth himself shall be abased; and he that humbleth himself shall be exalted"* Luke 18:10-14.

Beyond forgiveness, there is cleansing – 1 John 1:7; *"If we confess our sins, he is faithful and just to forgive us our sins, and to cleanse us from all unrighteousness"* 1 John 1:9.

Practical:

1. What are you going to do to increase your prayer life? When are you going to do it? _____

    _____

    _____

2. How often do you believe Jesus prayed? Why did He pray? _____

    _____

    _____

3. When have you heard someone use the four words of "The Devil's Prayer"? When have you uttered

    them? _____

    _____

    Discuss with a friend or spouse what you can do about it now.

Repeat this prayer out loud:

Father, forgive me for prayerlessness and for the times I've actually said "The Devil's Prayer." I choose today to become a man of prayer. Help me fulfill this decision as I press into You. In Jesus' Name. Amen.

For Further Study

Love God's Word – If a person loves truth, he will make it a part of his life – *"Receive with meekness the engrafted word, which is able to save your souls. But be ye doers of the word, and not hearers only, deceiving your own selves"* James 1:21, 22; Psalm 119:97; Titus 2:7.

Self Test *Lesson 10*

1. Define "prayer abuse." _____

2. Prayer is important to time management. ____ True ____ False

3. How does God's Word tell us we can add time to our days? _____

4. List four elements to success in life.

   a. _____ b. _____ c. _____ d. _____

5. Meditation is the _____ of _____.

6. Why is meditation on God's Word and time in prayer so necessary? _____

   _____

   _____

7. What prayer is found in Luke 11:1-4? _____

8. What are the four words of "The Devil's Prayer"? _____

9. You become intimate with the one …

   _____ whom you pray, _____ whom you pray and _____ whom you pray.

10. The practice of lifting people up in prayer produces spiritual _____.

11. You don't get good then get to God; you get to God, and He _____!

Keep this test for your records.

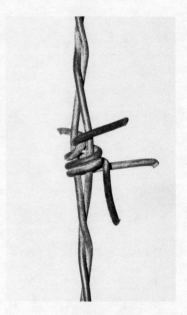

Lesson 11
Wake Up, Dad!

Lesson 11
Wake Up, Dad!

A. Read Daniel 11.

1. Hearing from God doesn't depend on age but on _____. *(page 145)*

2. Daniel was believed to be how old when he was carried away into Babylon? *(circle one) (page 145)*

   a. 8   b. 15   c. 22

3. One characteristic of strength is: *(circle one) (page 145)*

   a. power   b. fierceness   c. resilience

4. The Bible never records Joseph or Daniel doing what? *(circle one) (page 146)*

   a. murmuring   b. persevering   c. adamantly rejecting something

5. The present is merely _____. *(page 146)*

For Further Study

Develop your own relationship with God – *"Even the Spirit of truth; whom the world cannot receive, because it seeth him not, neither knoweth him: but ye know him: for he dwelleth with you, and shall be in you"* John 14:17. You are never too young to hear from God. Hearing from God doesn't depend on age but on relationship – *"My sheep hear my voice, and I know them, and they follow me"* John 10:27.

Friendship with God is based on relationship, not religion – *"I don't want your sacrifices—I want your love; I don't want want your offerings—I want you to know me"* Hosea 6:6 TLB; *"The Lord is good, a strong hold in the day of trouble; and he knoweth them that trust in him"* Nahum 1:7.

Write down what God has taught you today and what He teaches you day by day in the future – Revelations 1:19.

Failure precedes success – 1 Samuel 30:1-20; 2 Samuel 2:4; *"But David found strength in the Lord his God"* 1 Samuel 30:6 NIV.

B. Never Too Soon to Start

1. Men must prepare their children today for the day when they will be called upon to live by *(circle one)* *(page 147)*

    a. their own wits.
    b. a new standard of morality.
    c. their own standards without parental support.

2. What does the Scripture say is a father's responsibility to his children? Write out Ephesians 6:4.

    _____

    _____

3. Identify some specific issues step-parents have to deal with. *(page 148)*

    a. _____   c. _____

    b. _____

4. Men are working harder to make less money than in years past. The inability to give time is doing what? *(page 149)* _____

    _____

For Further Study

Teach and train – *"Impress them on your children"* Deuteronomy 6:5-9 NIV; *"Teach them to your children"* Deuteronomy 11:18-21 NIV; Colossians 3:16; 1 Thessalonians 4:1-8.
Who should teach – Fathers and mothers – Proverbs 1:8-9; 4:1; 6:20-24; Spiritual leaders – Malachi 2:7; The righteous – Proverbs 10:21; Elders – 1 Timothy 1:18; 4:14
Father's responsibility for children – *"Fathers, do not irritate and provoke your children to anger [do not exasperate them to resentment], but rear them [tenderly] in the training and discipline and the counsel and admonition of the Lord"* Ephesians 6:4 AMP; *"Fathers, do not provoke or irritate or fret your children [do not be hard on them or harass them], lest they become discouraged and sullen and morose and feel inferior and frustrated [Do not break their spirit.]"* Colossians 3:21 AMP; 1 Timothy 3:4, 12; *"And, ye fathers, provoke not your children to wrath: but bring them up in the nurture and admonition of the Lord"* Ephesians 6:4.
What to teach – *"Set an example … in speech, in life, in love, in faith and in purity"* 1 Timothy 4:11-13 NIV; Titus 2:2-8.

C. The Evidences of Love

 1. Write out John 15:13. _____

 _____

 2. God's love is unconditional, _____ and _____. *(page 151)*

 3. List the three evidences of love. *(page 151)*

 a. _____   c. _____

 b. _____

D. The Provisions of Love

 1. What are the provisions of love? *(page 152)*

 a. _____   b. _____   c. _____

 2. When a woman marries a man and takes his name, she becomes identified with what? *(circle one)* *(page 152)*

 a. his money   b. his character   c. his past

 3. Loss of _____ is the underlying cause of most troubled marriages. *(fill in the blank)* *(page 152)*

 respect   a job   a mother-in-law

 4. What is the best "covering" a man can give his wife? *(page 152)* _____

For Further Study

Love is invisible; giving is visible – John 3:16; *"Greater love hath no man than this, that a man lay down his life for his friends"* John 15:13; Honor is invisible; obedience is visible – Luke 6:46; The degree of invisible love is evidenced by the degree of visible giving – 1 John 3:16. Unity results from love – Colossians 3:14.

Selflessness of the Trinity – *"But God commendeth His love toward us, in that, while we were yet sinners, Christ died for us"* Romans 5:8.

Identity – *"Behold, what manner of love the Father hath bestowed upon us, that we should be called the sons of God"* 1 John 3:1; Isaiah 62:12.

Security – Genesis 2:24; Proverbs 18:10; Mark 10:9

Stability – *"I have set the Lord always before me. Because he is at my right hand, I will not be shaken"* Psalm 16:8 NIV; *"He only is my rock and my salvation; he is my defence; I shall not be greatly moved"* Psalm 62:2.

5. A wife's security is primarily in her home. *(page 153)* _____ True _____ False

6. A husband's provisions are to be food, clothing and shelter and what else? *(page 153)*

    a. _____ b. _____ c. _____

7. How does a man provide a legacy for his family? *(page 153)* _____

    _____

8. **In your own words,** why is "stability" in our lives as men so important to our wives? *(page 154)*

    _____

    _____

    _____

9. What actions by a husband contribute to a lack of stability? *(page 154)* _____

    _____

    _____

10. What effect do these have on children? *(page 154)* _____

    _____

For Further Study

The characteristics of the kingdom emanate from the character of the king – Hosea 4:9.

Personality is not the same as character – Proverbs 26:23; Personality is after the outward man and is temporal – 1 Samuel 16:7. Character and the honor of God – Obedience to His Word honors God, disobedience dishonors Him – 1 Samuel 15:22-23; Proverbs 14:2. A man who has learned to honor God privately will show good character in his decisions – Psalm 119:101, 102, 104. God commits to character, not to talent – *"And the things you have heard me say in the presence of many witnesses entrust to reliable men who will also be qualified to teach others"* 2 Timothy 2:2; Matthew 25:21; Luke 16:10.

Ways to earn respect – *"Husbands, in the same way be considerate as you live with your wives, and treat them with respect"* 1 Peter 3:7 NIV; Ephesians 6:4; 1 John 3:18.

Choose to have a good name – *"A good name is better than fine perfume"* Ecclesiastes 7:1 NIV; *"A good name is rather to be chosen than great riches, and loving favour rather than silver and gold"* Proverbs 22:1.

E.   The Current Crisis

   1.   More and more women today are choosing to have children without _____.
(page 156)

   2.   Why is this? *(page 156)* _____

_____

   3.   Gangs provide these four things that are the father's responsibility: *(page 157)*

     a. _____   c. _____

     b. _____   d. _____

   4.   Name the four basic desires in life that gangs fulfill. *(page 157)*

     a. _____   c. _____

     b. _____   d. _____

   5.   Who is to provide those four things? *(page 157)* _____

   6.   What is family life to provide? *(page 158)*

_____

For Further Study

A man's name is only as good as his word. Prepare your name to have a good character – Proverbs 12:17; 22:1. Aspire to be a man of your word – *"For in many ways we offend all. If any man offend not in word, the same is a perfect man, and able also to bridle the whole body"* James 3:2; The power of words – *"The tongue has the power of life and death, and those who love it will eat its fruit"* Proverbs 18:21 NIV; Psalms 15:1-4; 119:130; Proverbs 6:2; 11:9; 12:6, 18, 25; 13:3; 15:4; Matthew 12:37; Romans 16:18; James 3:9.
Keep your word – Psalm 34:12, 13; John 10:10. The word releases the spirit – Proverbs 23:7.
Inconsistency is a mark of immaturity and takes a toll on those around us – Proverbs 25:19; James 1:8; 4:8.
Whether or not we mature affects everyone around us – *"We are all parts of one body"* Ephesians 4:4 TLB.
The desire to belong is basic – Genesis 2:18. It causes pressure to go along with others – Proverbs 1:10, 15.
Rejection is one of life's cruelest blows – Isaiah 53:3; John 1:11. Rejection is often the root of feelings of suicide – 1 Kings 19:4, 10. People need to feel loved and valued – 1 Corinthians 9:7-10; 1 Timothy 5:18.

Practical:

1. Read Jeremiah 6:14. How does this relate to the saying "The spouse is always the last to know"? In what way are you guilty of saying "peace" when there is none?

   _____

   _____

   _____

2. Why do you think women today are choosing to have children without husbands or fathers?

   _____

   _____

   _____

   _____

3. When was the last time you took your wife away alone? Plan now, book now, schedule now.

Repeat this prayer out loud:

Father, I repent for every way in which I have failed my family. I receive Your forgiveness and Your guidance to help me do right for them. Help me to ask for forgiveness and to change where needed. Amen.

For Further Study

As long as a man's words live, he lives – *"There is living truth in what a good man says"* Proverbs 10:11 TLB. God's Words sown into a life – John 6:63; 1 Peter 1:23; Man's words sown into a life – Proverbs 11:30, 15:4
The son's responsibility is to honor his father – Proverbs 20:20; Ephesians 6:2. Sons are to submit to their father's authority in the Lord – Colossians 3:20. Sons are not to allow their father's sins to ruin their lives – Hebrews 12:15. Sons are to make sure their hearts are clean before God concerning their fathers, forgiving them of all offenses, sins and neglect – Ephesians 4:31-32.
The importance of the father-son relationship – Proverbs 17:6; 20:7; *"Reverence for God gives a man deep strength; his children have a place of refuge and security"* Proverbs 14:26 TLB.

Self Test *Lesson 11*

1. The Bible never records Joseph or Daniel doing what? *(circle one)*

   a. murmuring   b. persevering   c. adamantly rejecting something

2. A man is to love his family, as God loves us, which is manifested in these three basic ways:

   a. Unconditional   b. _____   c. _____

3. Name the three evidences of love.

   a. _____   b. desire to benefit the one loved   c. _____

4. What are three major provisions of love? a. identity   b. _____   c. _____

5. Loss of _____ is the underlying cause of most troubled marriages.

6. What groups can we identify as "counterfeit families"? _____

7. The father's responsibility is to provide these four:

   a. intimacy   b. _____   c. _____   d. _____

8. Name the four basic desires that gangs fulfill.

   a. _____   b. _____   c. _____   d. _____

Keep this test for your records.

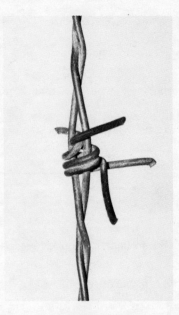

Lesson 12
A Decade of Daring

Lesson 12
A Decade of Daring

A. Read Daniel 12.

    1. The book of Daniel consists greatly of what? *(page 161)* _____

    2. Name two things prophets do. *(page 162)*

        a. _____   b. _____

    3. By honoring Daniel, who received honor? *(page 162)* _____

B. What's Happening Now?

    1. List some of the things the Bible predicts about the last days. *(page 163)*

    _____

    _____

    _____

For Further Study

Prophets emphasize the specific Word God has given them – *"The lion hath roared, who will not fear? the Lord God hath spoken, who can but prophesy?"* Amos 3:8; *"And Micaiah said, As the Lord liveth, what the Lord saith unto me, that will I speak"* 1 Kings 22:14; *"The prophet that hath a dream, let him tell a dream; and he that hath my word, let him speak my word faithfully"* Jeremiah 23:28; *"Speak unto all the cities of Judah … all the words that I command thee to speak unto them; diminish not a word"* Jeremiah 26:2.

The last days – *"Perilous times shall come. For men shall be lovers of their own selves, covetous … trucebreakers, false accusers … despisers of those that are good … lovers of pleasures more than lovers of God; Having a form of godliness, but denying the power thereof: from such turn away. For of this sort are they which creep into houses, and lead captive silly women laden with sins, led away with divers lusts, Ever learning, and never able to come to the knowledge of the truth"* 2 Timothy 3:1-7.

2. Name three characteristics of the "spirit of the world" in the last days. *(page 163)*

   a. _____

   b. _____

   c. _____

3. What was one of the characteristics that presaged Babylon's downfall? *(page 164)*

   _____

   _____

4. Often leaders testify to a born-again theology, but they practice what? *(page 164)*

   _____

5. What the world cannot control, it will _____ and _____.
   What the church cannot control, it will _____ and
   _____. What men cannot control, they will _____
   and _____. *(page 165)*

For Further Study

Failure of courage – *"The mighty men of Babylon have forborne to fight, they have remained in their holds: their might hath failed; they became as women: they have burned her dwellingplaces; her bars are broken"* Jeremiah 51:30.

Last days – *"And even as they did not like to retain God in their knowledge, God gave them over to a reprobate mind, to do those things which are not convenient; Being filled with all unrighteousness, fornication, wickedness, covetousness, maliciousness; full of envy, murder, debate, deceit, malignity; whisperers, Backbiters, haters of God, despiteful, proud, boasters, inventors of evil things, disobedient to parents, Without understanding, covenantbreakers, without natural affection, implacable, unmerciful: Who knowing the judgment of God, that they which commit such things are worthy of death, not only do the same, but have pleasure in them that do them"* Romans 1:28-32; *"Knowing this first, that there shall come in the last days scoffers, walking after their own lusts"* 2 Peter 3:3; Romans 2:5-6.

6.   Write out 2 Peter 3:3.

_____

_____

7.   God always starts on a positive. God will end the history of man on earth, not with a _____,

but with a _____. *(page 166)*

C.   Judgment Day Is Coming

1.   The rise of the worship of evil is actually what? *(page 167)*

_____

_____

2.   What should be our proper response to wrongdoing? *(page 167)* _____

For Further Study

Sin's deception – Sin promises to serve, but it creates bondage – *"Jesus answered them, Verily, verily, I say unto you, Whosoever committeth sin is the servant of sin"* John 8:34; 2 Peter 2:19; *"When the woman saw that the tree was good for food … she took of the fruit thereof, and did eat, and gave also unto her husband … and he did eat. And the eyes of them both were opened, and they knew that they were naked; and they sewed fig leaves together, and made themselves aprons. And they heard the voice of the Lord God walking in the garden … and Adam and his wife hid themselves from the presence of the Lord God"* Genesis 3:6-8.

God's indignation and wrath – *"And the Lord rooted them out of their land in anger, and in wrath, and in great indignation, and cast them into another land, as it is this day"* Deuteronomy 29:28; Isaiah 30:27, 30; 34:2; *"And when ye see this, your heart shall rejoice, and your bones shall flourish like an herb: and the hand of the Lord shall be known toward his servants, and his indignation toward his enemies"* Isaiah 66:14; Numbers 11:33; 16:46; Romans 1:18, 2:8.

3. God gives seven principles for the judgment of this world. They are: *(pages 167-168)*

    a. _____

    b. _____

    _____

    c. _____

    _____

    d. _____

    e. _____

    _____

    f. _____

    _____

    _____

    g. _____

4. In Hosea's prophecies, God described _____ reasons for the downfall of Israel. The last and worst in God's eyes was what? *(page 169)* _____

5. Give some modern examples of this sin. *(pages 169-170)*

    _____

    _____

For Further Study

Judgment of God – *"But we are sure that the judgment of God is according to truth against them which commit such things ... But after thy hardness and impenitent heart treasurest up unto thyself wrath against the day of wrath and revelation of the righteous judgment of God; Who will render to every man according to his deeds ... For there is no respect of persons with God ... For not the hearers of the law are just before God, but the doers of the law shall be justified ... In the day when God shall judge the secrets of men by Jesus Christ according to my gospel ... But he is a Jew, which is one inwardly; and circumcision is that of the heart, in the spirit, and not in the letter; whose praise is not of men, but of God"* Romans 2:2, 5, 6, 11, 13, 16, 29; The Book of Hosea.

D.   Who Christians Really Are

   1.   Read 1 Peter 2:9.

   2.   Christians are "_____ - _____" ones.   *(page 171)*

   3.   A Christian's purpose is to _____. *(page 171)*

   4.   Jesus said that His Kingdom was not _____. *(page 171)*

   5.   Social conscience, philanthropy and benevolence have traditionally started where? *(page 171)*

   _____

E.   What Christians Really Do
   1.   What is the "greatest act of philanthropy"? *(page 172)* _____

   _____

   2.   What is the highest and most noble calling on earth? *(page 174)*

   _____

   3.   This world is in transition, crisis and confusion. The people of today need a _____.

        They need a _____. *(page 176)*

   4.   The love of the _____ is the _____ of _____

        _____. *(page 177)*

For Further Study

"*But ye are a chosen generation, a royal priesthood, an holy nation, a peculiar people; that ye should show forth the praises of him who hath called you out of darkness into his marvellous light*" 1 Peter 2:9.

The ministry of reconciliation – "*And all things are of God, who hath reconciled us to himself by Jesus Christ, and hath given to us the ministry of reconciliation*" 2 Corinthians 5:18.

The Christian's purpose – "*Go ye therefore, and teach all nations, baptizing them in the name of the Father, and of the Son, and of the Holy Ghost*" Matthew 28:19; "*And he said unto them, Go ye into all the world, and preach the gospel to every creature*" Mark 16:15.

The Kingdom – "*Jesus answered, My kingdom is not of this world: if my kingdom were of this world, then would my servants fight, that I should not be delivered to the Jews: but now is my kingdom not from hence*" John 18:36.

Roots of benevolence – Acts 2:44, 45; 4:35; Ephesians 4:28; 1 John 3:17

Practical:

1.   Discuss the characteristics of the "spirit of the world" in the last days. Where do you see those characteristics?

2.   Name instances where you have personally responded to the world with a social conscience, philanthropy and/or benevolence: _____

3.   Discuss with your spouse or friend: Would you be willing for your son or daughter to receive "the highest and most noble calling on earth"?

Repeat this prayer out loud:

Father, I have learned about myself. I need far more of Your work within me than I ever realized. I accept Your intervention in my life. I realize this world will not last forever, that I have friends and family who need to know You and that the entire world is waiting for a man who will live an uncompromising life of boldness for Christ. I am willing to be that man. I am willing to die to myself in order to bring others into eternal life. Lead me and guide me, I pray, and help me be the man You created me to be. In Christ's Name, I pray. Amen.

For Further Study

The highest calling – *"And how shall they preach, except they be sent?"* Romans 10:15; 1 Thessalonians 1:5; *"Paul, a servant of Jesus Christ, called to be an apostle, separated unto the gospel of God"* Romans 1:1; *"Paul, called to be an apostle of Jesus Christ through the will of God"* 1 Corinthians 1:1, 26; 2 Thessalonians 1:11; 2 Timothy 1:9.
Find a godly pastor who can help you and be your example – Philippians 3:17, 18. A pastor who loves truth will produce a congregation that loves truth – 1 Thessalonians 1:6, 7.
Examples of men who honored God: Joseph became second in command to Pharaoh – Genesis 39:7-12; 41:39, 40; Mordecai was elevated by God to prime minister – Esther 2:21, 22; 10:3; Shadrach, Meshach and Abednego were delivered and promoted – Daniel 3:16-18, 30; See also 1 Samuel 2:30, Psalm 91:14-15; John 12:26.
Set an example – 1 Timothy 4:12; James 5:10; 1 Peter 2:21.

Self Test *Lesson 12*

1. Lawlessness, impenitence and masochism are three characteristics of what?

    _____

2. What the world cannot control, it will _____ and _____.

3. The Lord always starts on a negative and finishes on a positive.   ____ True   ____ False

4. Judgment will be according to intentions, not deeds.   ____ True   ____ False

5. The Holocaust in Germany during World War II was a type of what? _____

6. Social conscience, philanthropy and benevolence have traditionally started where?

    _____

7. What is the "greatest act of philanthropy"? _____

    _____

8. What is the highest and most noble call on earth? _____

9. The world today needs men who will live uncompromising lives in the midst of

    _____.

Keep this test for your records.

Final Exam

1. Did God create men to be leaders and heroes? ____ Yes ____ No

2. Name the book of the Bible where we read *"Just as my mouth can taste good food, so my mind tastes truth when I hear it."* _____

3. The lowest level of knowledge is assumption. ____ True ____ False

4. Men without an organized system of thought will always be what? *(circle one)*

   a. at the mercy of men who have one   b. poor students

5. Fame can come in a _____. Greatness comes with _____.

6. Perseverance will always outlast persecution. ____ True ____ False

7. A person's belief system holds or creates the greatest potential for good or harm in life. ____ True ____ False

8. Which is more important? *(circle one)*

   a. to pray for opportunities to come   b. to pray to be ready for opportunities when they do come

9. Who is the counterfeit trinity?

   a. _____   b. _____   c. _____

10. A man's companions say much about his what? *(circle one)*

   a. alma mater   b. life   c. character

Final Exam

11. Match the words below to the correct description:

   a. enthusiasm   _____ an attitude

   b. optimism   _____ a substance

   c. faith   _____ an emotion

12. A young man must reach the age of accountability before he will ever hear from God. ____ True   ____ False

13. God has no faith in mankind.   ____ True   ____ False

14. Being nice is not always being loving.   ____ True   ____ False

15. To eliminate guilt, what must be done? *(circle one)*

   a. blame someone else   b. hold on to it   c. eliminate the cause

16. We can trust the will of God, because God always wills and works toward our highest good.
   ____ True   ____ False

17. Life is lived on _____ and arrived at in _____.

18. Modern church movements have unfortunately been marred in that they tended to omit the cross and
   ignore repentance.   ____ True   ____ False

19. No cross, no _____.

20. Satan has the power to make us sin.   ____ True   ____ False

21. God's intent is for sermons to set us free.   ____ True   ____ False

22. God's Word is His _____.

Final Exam

23. God's Word is magnified above His _____.

24. To be conformed to the image of Christ, our _____ must conform to God's Word.

25. Our name is only as good as what? _____

26. In the parable of the sower, Jesus said Satan comes immediately to steal the word that was sown. How does a "word" get stolen?

    _____

    _____

    _____

27. We are to forgive: *(circle one)*
    a. when we feel able.   b. as Christ forgave us.   c. only if others say they are sorry.

28. Forgiveness _____. *(fill in the blank)*
    opens   closes   disappoints

29. Forgiveness is always something that is earned.   ____ True   ____ False

30. Even though God will forgive us, He will still bring back to remembrance our sins in order to convict us.
    ____ True   ____ False

31. If we don't forgive, even when God has forgiven, we make ourselves _____.

32. Forgiveness needs to be given in the same spirit in which it was asked.   ____ True   ____ False

33. What are "sins of omission"? _____

Final Exam

34. Lower morality leads to higher _____. *(fill in the blank)*
    mortality   promiscuity   crime

35. Who brought absolute morality into the world? _____

36. No man becomes immoral in deed without first becoming immoral in _____.

37. There is no seduction without: *(circle one)*
    a. sin   b. flirtation   c. revealing clothes

38. Reading the Bible: *(circle all that apply)*

    a. gives knowledge to the intellect.   c. programs the conscience.

    b. inscribes God's commandments upon the heart.   d. fails to change a man.

39. Circle the foundational "bedrocks" on which to build a Christian life.
    a. what people say   d. good advice   g. reading the Bible
    b. reading articles   e. praying   h. listening to Christian radio
    c. fasting   f. Christian television   i. human wisdom

40. Counselors determine the _____ of kings.

41. Weakness ascends when _____. *(fill in the blank)*
    strength abdicates   liberals win   wisdom prevails

42. Meditation is the _____ of _____.

43. What are the four words of "The Devil's Prayer"? _____

44. You become intimate with the one ...

    _____ whom you pray   _____ whom you pray and   _____ whom you pray.

DETACH HERE

Final Exam

45. Since prayer doesn't come naturally, are men excused from learning to pray? ____ Yes ____ No

46. You don't get good then get to God, you get God, and He _____!

47. The Bible never records Joseph or Daniel doing what? *(circle one)*

    a. murmuring   b. persevering   c. adamantly rejecting something

48. A man is to love his family as God loves us, which is:

    a. unconditionally   b. _____   c. _____

49. What are three major provisions of love?

    a. identity   b. _____   c. _____

50. The father's responsibility is to provide these four:

    a. intimacy   b. _____   c. _____   d. _____

51. The Lord always starts on a negative and finishes on a positive. ____ True ____ False

52. Social conscience, philanthropy and benevolence have traditionally started where?

    _____

53. What is the "greatest act of philanthropy"?

    _____

DETACH HERE

Final Exam

54. Short essay: The Bible says, in Revelation 3:16, that if you are lukewarm, God will "spew" you out of His mouth. Why is being lukewarm such a sin, and what is the antidote? Use examples from your own life and from the book.

_____

_____

_____

_____

_____

_____

_____

_____

_____

Name _____

Address _____

City _____ State _____ Zip _____

Telephone a.m. _____ p.m. _____

Email address _____

The Final Exam is required to be "commissioned."

CMN
WORLDWIDE

For more information, contact
Christian Men's Network | P.O. Box 93478 | Southlake, TX 76092
ChristianMensNetwork.com | office@ChristianMensNetwork.com 817-437-4888

DETACH HERE

Basic Daily Bible Reading

Read Proverbs each morning for wisdom, Psalms each evening for courage. Make copies of this chart and keep it in your Bible to mark off as you read. If you are just starting the habit of Bible reading, be aware that longer translations or paraphrases (such as Amplified and Living) will take longer to read each day. As you start, it is okay to read only one of the chapters in Psalms each night, instead of the many listed. Mark your chart so you'll remember which ones you haven't read.

NOTE: The chronological chart following has the rest of the chapters of Psalms that are not listed here. By using both charts together, you will cover the entire book of Psalms.

Day of Month	Proverbs	Psalms	Day of Month	Proverbs	Psalms
1	1	1, 2, 4, 5, 6	18	18	82, 83, 84, 85
2	2	7, 8, 9	19	19	87, 88, 91, 92
3	3	10, 11, 12, 13, 14, 15	20	20	93, 94, 95, 97
4	4	16, 17, 19, 20	21	21	98, 99, 100, 101, 103
5	5	21, 22, 23	22	22	104, 108
6	6	24, 25, 26, 27	23	23	109, 110, 111
7	7	28, 29, 31, 32	24	24	112, 113, 114, 115, 117
8	8	33, 35	25	25	119:1-56
9	9	36, 37	26	26	119:57-112
10	10	38, 39, 40	27	27	119:113-176
11	11	41, 42, 43, 45, 46	28	28	120, 121, 122, 124, 130, 131, 133, 134
12	12	47, 48, 49, 50			
13	13	53, 55, 58, 61, 62	29	29	135, 136, 138
14	14	64, 65, 66, 67	30	30	139, 140, 141, 143
15	15	68, 69	31	31	144, 145, 146, 148, 150
16	16	70, 71, 73			
17	17	75, 76, 77, 81			

Chronological Annual Bible Reading

This schedule follows the events of the Bible chronologically and can be used with any translation or paraphrase of the Bible. Each day has an average of 77 verses of Scripture. If you follow this annually, along with your Daily Bible Reading, by your third year, you will recognize where you are and what is going to happen next. By your fifth year, you will understand the Scriptural background and setting for any reference spoken of in a message or book. At that point, the Word will become more like "meat" to you and less like "milk." Once you understand the basic stories and what happens on the surface, God can reveal to you the layers of meaning beneath. So, make copies of this chart to keep in your Bible and mark off as you read. And start reading—it's the greatest adventure in life!

Some notes:

1. Some modern translations don't have verses numbered (such as The Message), so they cannot be used with this chart. Also, if you are just starting the Bible, be aware that longer translations or paraphrases (such as Amplified and Living) tend to take longer to read each day.

2. The Daily Bible Reading chart covers the Proverbs and the chapters of Psalms that are not listed here. By using both charts together, you will cover the entire books of Psalms and Proverbs along with the rest of the Bible.

3. The chronology of Scripture is obvious in some cases, educated guesswork in others. The placement of Job, for example, is purely conjecture since there is no consensus among Bible scholars as to its date or place. For the most part, however, chronological reading helps the reader, since it places stories that have duplicated information, or prophetic utterances elsewhere in Scripture, within the same reading sequence.

HOW TO READ SCRIPTURE NOTATIONS:

Book chapter: verse. (Mark 15:44 means the book of Mark, chapter 15, verse 44.)

Book chapter; chapter (Mark 15; 16; 17 means the book of Mark, chapters 15, 16, 17.)

Books continue the same until otherwise noted. (2 Kings 22; 23:1-28; Jeremiah 20 means the book of 2 Kings, chapter 22, the book of 2 Kings, chapter 23, verses 1-28; then the book of Jeremiah, chapter 20.)

MAJORING IN MEN®

1	Jan 1	Genesis 1; 2; 3
2	Jan 2	Genesis 4; 5; 6
3	Jan 3	Genesis 7; 8; 9
4	Jan 4	Genesis 10; 11; 12
5	Jan 5	Genesis 13; 14; 15; 16
6	Jan 6	Genesis 17; 18; 19:1-29
7	Jan 7	Genesis 19:30-38; 20; 21
8	Jan 8	Genesis 22; 23; 24:1-31
9	Jan 9	Genesis 24:32-67; 25
10	Jan 10	Genesis 26; 27
11	Jan 11	Genesis 28; 29; 30:1-24
12	Jan 12	Genesis 30:25-43; 31
13	Jan 13	Genesis 32; 33; 34
14	Jan 14	Genesis 35; 36
15	Jan 15	Genesis 37; 38; 39
16	Jan 16	Genesis 40; 41
17	Jan 17	Genesis 42; 43
18	Jan 18	Genesis 44; 45
19	Jan 19	Genesis 46; 47; 48
20	Jan 20	Genesis 49; 50; Exodus 1
21	Jan 21	Exodus 2; 3; 4
22	Jan 22	Exodus 5; 6; 7
23	Jan 23	Exodus 8; 9
24	Jan 24	Exodus 10; 11; 12
25	Jan 25	Exodus 13; 14; 15
26	Jan 26	Exodus 16; 17; 18
27	Jan 27	Exodus 19; 20; 21
28	Jan 28	Exodus 22; 23; 24
29	Jan 29	Exodus 25; 26
30	Jan 30	Exodus 27; 28; 29:1-28
31	Jan 31	Exodus 29:29-46; 30; 31
32	Feb 1	Exodus 32; 33; 34
33	Feb 2	Exodus 35; 36
34	Feb 3	Exodus 37; 38
35	Feb 4	Exodus 39; 40
36	Feb 5	Leviticus 1; 2; 3; 4
37	Feb 6	Leviticus 5; 6; 7
38	Feb 7	Leviticus 8; 9; 10
39	Feb 8	Leviticus 11; 12; 13:1-37
40	Feb 9	Leviticus 13:38-59; 14
41	Feb 10	Leviticus 15; 16
42	Feb 11	Leviticus 17; 18; 19
43	Feb 12	Leviticus 20; 21; 22:1-16
44	Feb 13	Leviticus 22:17-33; 23
45	Feb 14	Leviticus 24; 25
46	Feb 15	Leviticus 26; 27
47	Feb 16	Numbers 1; 2
48	Feb 17	Numbers 3; 4:1-20
49	Feb 18	Numbers 4:21-49; 5; 6
50	Feb 19	Numbers 7
51	Feb 20	Numbers 8; 9; 10
52	Feb 21	Numbers 11; 12; 13
53	Feb 22	Numbers 14; 15
54	Feb 23	Numbers 16; 17
55	Feb 24	Numbers 18; 19; 20
56	Feb 25	Numbers 21; 22
57	Feb 26	Numbers 23; 24; 25
58	Feb 27	Numbers 26; 27
59	Feb 28	Numbers 28; 29; 30
60	Mar 1	Numbers 31; 32:1-27
61	Mar 2	Numbers 32:28-42; 33
62	Mar 3	Numbers 34; 35; 36
63	Mar 4	Deuteronomy 1; 2
64	Mar 5	Deuteronomy 3; 4
65	Mar 6	Deuteronomy 5; 6; 7
66	Mar 7	Deuteronomy 8; 9; 10
67	Mar 8	Deuteronomy 11; 12; 13
68	Mar 9	Deuteronomy 14; 15; 16
69	Mar 10	Deuteronomy 17; 18; 19; 20
70	Mar 11	Deuteronomy 21; 22; 23
71	Mar 12	Deuteronomy 24; 25; 26; 27
72	Mar 13	Deuteronomy 28
73	Mar 14	Deuteronomy 29; 30; 31
74	Mar 15	Deuteronomy 32; 33
75	Mar 16	Deuteronomy 34; Psalm 90; Joshua 1; 2
76	Mar 17	Joshua 3; 4; 5; 6
77	Mar 18	Joshua 7; 8; 9
78	Mar 19	Joshua 10; 11
79	Mar 20	Joshua 12; 13; 14
80	Mar 21	Joshua 15; 16
81	Mar 22	Joshua 17; 18; 19:1-23
82	Mar 23	Joshua 19:24-51; 20; 21
83	Mar 24	Joshua 22; 23; 24
84	Mar 25	Judges 1; 2; 3:1-11
85	Mar 26	Judges 3:12-31; 4; 5
86	Mar 27	Judges 6; 7
87	Mar 28	Judges 8; 9
88	Mar 29	Judges 10; 11; 12
89	Mar 30	Judges 13; 14; 15
90	Mar 31	Judges 16; 17; 18
91	Apr 1	Judges 19; 20
		[You have completed 1/4 of the Bible!]
92	Apr 2	Judges 21; Job 1; 2; 3
93	Apr 3	Job 4; 5; 6
94	Apr 4	Job 7; 8; 9
95	Apr 5	Job 10; 11; 12
96	Apr 6	Job 13; 14; 15
97	Apr 7	Job 16; 17; 18; 19
98	Apr 8	Job 20; 21
99	Apr 9	Job 22; 23; 24
100	Apr 10	Job 25; 26; 27; 28
101	Apr 11	Job 29; 30; 31
102	Apr 12	Job 32; 33; 34
103	Apr 13	Job 35; 36; 37
104	Apr 14	Job 38; 39
105	Apr 15	Job 40; 41; 42
106	Apr 16	Ruth 1; 2; 3
107	Apr 17	Ruth 4; 1 Samuel 1; 2
108	Apr 18	1 Samuel 3; 4; 5; 6
109	Apr 19	1 Samuel 7; 8; 9
110	Apr 20	1 Samuel 10; 11; 12; 13
111	Apr 21	1 Samuel 14; 15
112	Apr 22	1 Samuel 16; 17
113	Apr 23	1 Samuel 18; 19; Psalm 59
114	Apr 24	1 Samuel 20; 21; Psalms 34; 56
115	Apr 25	1 Samuel 22; 23, Psalms 52; 142
116	Apr 26	1 Samuel 24; 25; 1 Chronicles 12:8-18; Psalm 57
117	Apr 27	1 Samuel 26; 27; 28; Psalms 54; 63
118	Apr 28	1 Samuel 29; 30; 31; 1 Chronicles 12:1-7; 12:19-22
119	Apr 29	1 Chronicles 10; 2 Samuel 1; 2
120	Apr 30	2 Samuel 3; 4; 1 Chronicles 11:1-9; 12:23-40
121	May 1	2 Samuel 5; 6; 1 Chronicles 13; 14
122	May 2	2 Samuel 22; 1 Chronicles 15
123	May 3	1 Chronicles 16; Psalm 18
124	May 4	2 Samuel 7; Psalms 96; 105
125	May 5	1 Chronicles 17; 2 Samuel 8; 9; 10
126	May 6	1 Chronicles 18; 19; Psalm 60; 2 Samuel 11
127	May 7	2 Samuel 12; 13; 1 Chronicles 20:1-3; Psalm 51
128	May 8	2 Samuel 14; 15
129	May 9	2 Samuel 16; 17; 18; Psalm 3
130	May 10	2 Samuel 19; 20; 21
131	May 11	2 Samuel 23:8-23
132	May 12	1 Chronicles 20:4-8; 11:10-25; 2 Samuel 23:24-39; 24
133	May 13	1 Chronicles 11:26-47; 21; 22
134	May 14	1 Chronicles 23; 24; Psalm 30
135	May 15	1 Chronicles 25; 26
136	May 16	1 Chronicles 27; 28; 29
137	May 17	1 Kings 1; 2:1-12; 2 Samuel 23:1-7
138	May 18	1 Kings 2:13-46; 3; 2 Chronicles 1:1-13
139	May 19	1 Kings 5; 6; 2 Chronicles 2
140	May 20	1 Kings 7; 2 Chronicles 3; 4
141	May 21	1 Kings 8; 2 Chronicles 5
142	May 22	1 Kings 9; 2 Chronicles 6; 7:1-10
143	May 23	1 Kings 10:1-13; 2 Chronicles 7:11-22; 8; 9:1-12; 1 Kings 4
144	May 24	1 Kings 10:14-29; 2 Chronicles 1:14-17; 9:13-28; Psalms 72; 127
145	May 25	Song of Solomon 1; 2; 3; 4; 5
146	May 26	Song of Solomon 6; 7; 8; 1 Kings 11:1-40
147	May 27	Ecclesiastes 1; 2; 3; 4
148	May 28	Ecclesiastes 5; 6; 7; 8
149	May 29	Ecclesiastes 9; 10; 11; 12; 1 Kings 11:41-43; 2 Chronicles 9:29-31
150	May 30	1 Kings 12; 2 Chronicles 10; 11
151	May 31	1 Kings 13; 14; 2 Chronicles 12
152	June 1	1 Kings 15; 2 Chronicles 13; 14; 15
153	June 2	1 Kings 16; 2 Chronicles 16; 17
154	June 3	1 Kings 17; 18; 19
155	June 4	1 Kings 20; 21
156	June 5	1 Kings 22; 2 Chronicles 18
157	June 6	2 Kings 1; 2; 2 Chronicles 19; 20; 21:1-3
158	June 7	2 Kings 3; 4
159	June 8	2 Kings 5; 6; 7
160	June 9	2 Kings 8; 9; 2 Chronicles 21:4-20
161	June 10	2 Chronicles 22; 23; 2 Kings 10; 11
162	June 11	Joel 1; 2; 3
163	June 12	2 Kings 12; 13; 2 Chronicles 24
164	June 13	2 Kings 14; 2 Chronicles 25; Jonah 1

MAJORING IN MEN®

165	June 14	Jonah 2; 3; 4; Hosea 1; 2; 3; 4
166	June 15	Hosea 5; 6; 7; 8; 9; 10
167	June 16	Hosea 11; 12; 13; 14
168	June 17	2 Kings 15:1-7; 2 Chronicles 26; Amos 1; 2; 3
169	June 18	Amos 4; 5; 6; 7
170	June 19	Amos 8; 9; 2 Kings 15:8-18; Isaiah 1
171	June 20	Isaiah 2; 3; 4; 2 Kings 15:19-38; 2 Chronicles 27
172	June 21	Isaiah 5; 6; Micah 1; 2; 3
173	June 22	Micah 4; 5; 6; 7; 2 Kings 16:1-18
174	June 23	2 Chronicles 28; Isaiah 7; 8
175	June 24	Isaiah 9; 10; 11; 12
176	June 25	Isaiah 13; 14; 15; 16
177	June 26	Isaiah 17; 18; 19; 20; 21
178	June 27	Isaiah 22; 23; 24; 25
179	June 28	Isaiah 26; 27; 28; 29
180	June 29	Isaiah 30; 31; 32; 33
181	June 30	Isaiah 34; 35; 2 Kings 18:1-8; 2 Chronicles 29
182	July 1	2 Chronicles 30; 31; 2 Kings 17; 2 Kings 16:19-20

[You have completed 1/2 of the Bible!]

183	July 2	2 Kings 18:9-37; 2 Chronicles 32:1-19; Isaiah 36
184	July 3	2 Kings 19; 2 Chronicles 32:20-23; Isaiah 37
185	July 4	2 Kings 20; 21:1-18; 2 Chronicles 32:24-33; Isaiah 38; 39
186	July 5	2 Chronicles 33:1-20; Isaiah 40; 41
187	July 6	Isaiah 42; 43; 44
188	July 7	Isaiah 45; 46; 47; 48
189	July 8	Isaiah 49; 50; 51; 52
190	July 9	Isaiah 53; 54; 55; 56; 57
191	July 10	Isaiah 58; 59; 60; 61; 62
192	July 11	Isaiah 63; 64; 65; 66
193	July 12	2 Kings 21:19-26; 2 Chronicles 33:21-25; 34:1-7; Zephaniah 1; 2; 3
194	July 13	Jeremiah 1; 2; 3
195	July 14	Jeremiah 4; 5
196	July 15	Jeremiah 6; 7; 8
197	July 16	Jeremiah 9; 10; 11
198	July 17	Jeremiah 12; 13; 14; 15
199	July 18	Jeremiah 16; 17; 18; 19
200	July 19	Jeremiah 20; 2 Kings 22; 23:1-28
201	July 20	2 Chronicles 34:8-33; 35:1-19; Nahum 1; 2; 3
202	July 21	2 Kings 23:29-37; 2 Chronicles 35:20-27; 36:1-5; Jeremiah 22:10-17; 26; Habakkuk 1
203	July 22	Habakkuk 2; 3; Jeremiah 46; 47; 2 Kings 24:1-4; 2 Chronicles 36:6-7
204	July 23	Jeremiah 25; 35; 36; 45
205	July 24	Jeremiah 48; 49:1-33
206	July 25	Daniel 1; 2
207	July 26	Jeremiah 22:18-30; 2 Kings 24:5-20; 2 Chronicles 36:8-12; Jeremiah 37:1-2; 52:1-3; 24; 29

208	July 27	Jeremiah 27; 28; 23
209	July 28	Jeremiah 50; 51:1-19
210	July 29	Jeremiah 51:20-64; 49:34-39; 34
211	July 30	Ezekiel 1; 2; 3; 4
212	July 31	Ezekiel 5; 6; 7; 8
213	Aug 1	Ezekiel 9; 10; 11; 12
214	Aug 2	Ezekiel 13, 14, 15, 16:1-34
215	Aug 3	Ezekiel 16:35-63; 17; 18
216	Aug 4	Ezekiel 19; 20
217	Aug 5	Ezekiel 21; 22
218	Aug 6	Ezekiel 23; 2 Kings 25:1; 2 Chronicles 36:13-16; Jeremiah 39:1; 52:4; Ezekiel 24
219	Aug 7	Jeremiah 21; 22:1-9; 32; 30
220	Aug 8	Jeremiah 31; 33; Ezekiel 25
221	Aug 9	Ezekiel 29:1-16; 30; 31; 26
222	Aug 10	Ezekiel 27; 28; Jeremiah 37:3-21
223	Aug 11	Jeremiah 38; 39:2-10; 52:5-30
224	Aug 12	2 Kings 25:2-22; 2 Chronicles 36:17-21; Jeremiah 39:11-18; 40:1-6; Lamentations 1
225	Aug 13	Lamentations 2; 3
226	Aug 14	Lamentations 4; 5; Obadiah; Jeremiah 40:7-16
227	Aug 15	Jeremiah 41; 42; 43; 44; 2 Kings 25:23-26
228	Aug 16	Ezekiel 33:21-33; 34; 35; 36
229	Aug 17	Ezekiel 37; 38; 39
230	Aug 18	Ezekiel 32; 33:1-20; Daniel 3
231	Aug 19	Ezekiel 40; 41
232	Aug 20	Ezekiel 42; 43; 44
233	Aug 21	Ezekiel 45; 46; 47
234	Aug 22	Ezekiel 48; 29:17-21; Daniel 4
235	Aug 23	Jeremiah 52:31-34; 2 Kings 25:27-30; Psalms 44; 74; 79
236	Aug 24	Psalms 80; 86; 89
237	Aug 25	Psalms 102; 106
238	Aug 26	Psalms 123; 137; Daniel 7; 8
239	Aug 27	Daniel 5; 9; 6
240	Aug 28	2 Chronicles 36:22-23; Ezra 1; 2
241	Aug 29	Ezra 3; 4:1-5; Daniel 10; 11
242	Aug 30	Daniel 12; Ezra 4:6-24; 5; 6:1-13; Haggai 1
243	Aug 31	Haggai 2; Zechariah 1; 2; 3
244	Sept 1	Zechariah 4; 5; 6; 7; 8
245	Sept 2	Ezra 6:14-22; Psalm 78
246	Sept 3	Psalms 107; 116; 118
247	Sept 4	Psalms 125; 126; 128; 129; 132; 147
248	Sept 5	Psalm 149; Zechariah 9; 10; 11; 12; 13
249	Sept 6	Zechariah 14; Esther 1; 2; 3
250	Sept 7	Esther 4; 5; 6; 7; 8
251	Sept 8	Esther 9; 10; Ezra 7; 8
252	Sept 9	Ezra 9; 10; Nehemiah 1
253	Sept 10	Nehemiah 2; 3; 4; 5
254	Sept 11	Nehemiah 6; 7
255	Sept 12	Nehemiah 8; 9; 10
256	Sept 13	Nehemiah 11; 12
257	Sept 14	Nehemiah 13; Malachi 1; 2; 3; 4

258	Sept 15	1 Chronicles 1; 2:1-35
259	Sept 16	1 Chronicles 2:36-55; 3; 4
260	Sept 17	1 Chronicles 5; 6:1-41
261	Sept 18	1 Chronicles 6:42-81; 7
262	Sept 19	1 Chronicles 8; 9
263	Sept 20	Matthew 1; 2; 3; 4
264	Sept 21	Matthew 5; 6
265	Sept 22	Matthew 7; 8
266	Sept 23	Matthew 9; 10
267	Sept 24	Matthew 11; 12
268	Sept 25	Matthew 13; 14
269	Sept 26	Matthew 15; 16
270	Sept 27	Matthew 17; 18; 19
271	Sept 28	Matthew 20; 21
272	Sept 29	Matthew 22; 23
273	Sept 30	Matthew 24; 25

[You have completed 3/4 of the Bible!]

274	Oct 1	Matthew 26; 27; 28
275	Oct 2	Mark 1; 2
276	Oct 3	Mark 3; 4
277	Oct 4	Mark 5; 6
278	Oct 5	Mark 7; 8:1-26
279	Oct 6	Mark 8:27-38; 9
280	Oct 7	Mark 10; 11
281	Oct 8	Mark 12; 13
282	Oct 9	Mark 14
283	Oct 10	Mark 15; 16
284	Oct 11	Luke 1
285	Oct 12	Luke 2; 3
286	Oct 13	Luke 4; 5
287	Oct 14	Luke 6; 7:1-23
288	Oct 15	Luke 7:24-50; 8
289	Oct 16	Luke 9
290	Oct 17	Luke 10; 11
291	Oct 18	Luke 12; 13
292	Oct 19	Luke 14; 15
293	Oct 20	Luke 16; 17
294	Oct 21	Luke 18; 19
295	Oct 22	Luke 20; 21
296	Oct 23	Luke 22
297	Oct 24	Luke 23; 24:1-28
298	Oct 25	Luke 24:29-53; John 1
299	Oct 26	John 2; 3; 4:1-23
300	Oct 27	John 4:24-54; 5; 6:1-7
301	Oct 28	John 6:8-71; 7:1-21
302	Oct 29	John 7:22-53; 8
303	Oct 30	John 9; 10
304	Oct 31	John 11; 12:1-28
305	Nov 1	John 12:29-50; 13; 14
306	Nov 2	John 15; 16; 17
307	Nov 3	John 18; 19:1-24
308	Nov 4	John 19:25-42; 20; 21
309	Nov 5	Acts 1; 2
310	Nov 6	Acts 3; 4
311	Nov 7	Acts 5; 6
312	Nov 8	Acts 7
313	Nov 9	Acts 8; 9
314	Nov 10	Acts 10
315	Nov 11	Acts 11
316	Nov 12	Acts 12; 13

MAJORING IN MEN®

317	Nov 13	Acts 14; 15; Galatians 1
318	Nov 14	Galatians 2; 3; 4
319	Nov 15	Galatians 5; 6; James 1
320	Nov 16	James 2; 3; 4; 5
321	Nov 17	Acts 16; 17
322	Nov 18	Acts 18:1-11; 1 Thessalonians 1; 2; 3; 4
323	Nov 19	1 Thessalonians 5; 2 Thessalonians 1; 2; 3
324	Nov 20	Acts 18:12-28; 19:1-22; 1 Corinthians 1
325	Nov 21	1 Corinthians 2; 3; 4; 5
326	Nov 22	1 Corinthians 6; 7; 8
327	Nov 23	1 Corinthians 9; 10; 11
328	Nov 24	1 Corinthians 12; 13; 14
329	Nov 25	1 Corinthians 15; 16
330	Nov 26	Acts 19:23-41; 20:1; 2 Corinthians 1; 2
331	Nov 27	2 Corinthians 3; 4; 5
332	Nov 28	2 Corinthians 6; 7; 8; 9
333	Nov 29	2 Corinthians 10; 11; 12
334	Nov 30	2 Corinthians 13; Romans 1; 2
335	Dec 1	Romans 3; 4; 5

336	Dec 2	Romans 6; 7; 8
337	Dec 3	Romans 9; 10; 11
338	Dec 4	Romans 12; 13; 14
339	Dec 5	Romans 15; 16
340	Dec 6	Acts 20:2-38; 21
341	Dec 7	Acts 22; 23
342	Dec 8	Acts 24; 25; 26
343	Dec 9	Acts 27; 28
344	Dec 10	Ephesians 1; 2; 3
345	Dec 11	Ephesians 4; 5; 6
346	Dec 12	Colossians 1; 2; 3
347	Dec 13	Colossians 4; Philippians 1; 2
348	Dec 14	Philippians 3; 4; Philemon
349	Dec 15	1 Timothy 1; 2; 3; 4
350	Dec 16	1 Timothy 5; 6; Titus 1; 2
351	Dec 17	Titus 3; 2 Timothy 1; 2; 3
352	Dec 18	2 Timothy 4; 1 Peter 1; 2
353	Dec 19	1 Peter 3; 4; 5; Jude
354	Dec 20	2 Peter 1; 2; 3; Hebrews 1
355	Dec 21	Hebrews 2; 3; 4; 5
356	Dec 22	Hebrews 6; 7; 8; 9
357	Dec 23	Hebrews 10; 11
358	Dec 24	Hebrews 12; 13; 2 John; 3 John

359	Dec 25	1 John 1; 2; 3; 4
360	Dec 26	1 John 5; Revelation 1; 2
361	Dec 27	Revelation 3; 4; 5; 6
362	Dec 28	Revelation 7; 8; 9; 10; 11
363	Dec 29	Revelation 12; 13; 14; 15
364	Dec 30	Revelation 16; 17; 18; 19
365	Dec 31	Revelation 20; 21; 22

*[You have completed the entire Bible
Congratulations!]*

DETACH HERE

MAJORING IN MEN® CURRICULUM

MANHOOD GROWTH PLAN

Order the corresponding workbook for each book, and study the first four Majoring In Men® Curriculum books in this order:

MAXIMIZED MANHOOD: Realize your need for God in every area of your life and start mending relationships with Christ and your family.

COURAGE: Make peace with your past, learn the power of forgiveness and the value of character. Let yourself be challenged to speak up for Christ to other men.

COMMUNICATION, SEX AND MONEY: Increase your ability to communicate, place the right values on sex and money in relationships, and greatly improve relationships, whether married or single.

STRONG MEN IN TOUGH TIMES: Reframe trials, battles and discouragement in light of Scripture and gain solid footing for business, career, and relational choices in the future.

Choose five of the following books to study next. When you have completed nine books, if you are not in men's group, you can find a Majoring In Men® group near you and become "commissioned" to minister to other men.

DARING: Overcome fear to live a life of daring ambition for Godly pursuits.

SEXUAL INTEGRITY: Recognize the sacredness of the sexual union, overcome mistakes and blunders and commit to righteousness in your sexuality.

UNIQUE WOMAN: Discover what makes a woman tick, from adolescence through maturity, to be able to minister to a spouse's uniqueness at any age.

NEVER QUIT: Take the ten steps for entering or leaving any situation, job, relationship or crisis in life.

REAL MAN: Discover the deepest meaning of Christlikeness and learn to exercise good character in times of stress, success or failure.

POWER OF POTENTIAL: Start making solid business and career choices based on Biblical principles while building core character that affects your entire life.

ABSOLUTE ANSWERS: Adopt practical habits and pursue Biblical solutions to overcome "prodigal problems" and secret sins that hinder both success and satisfaction with life.

TREASURE: Practice Biblical solutions and principles on the job to find treasures such as the satisfaction of exercising integrity and a job well done.

IRRESISTIBLE HUSBAND: Avoid common mistakes that sabotage a relationship and learn simple solutions and good habits to build a marriage that will consistently increase in intensity for decades.

MAJORING IN MEN® CURRICULUM

CHURCH GROWTH PLAN

STRONG - SUSTAINABLE - SYNERGISTIC

THREE PRACTICAL PHASES TO A POWERFUL MEN'S MOVEMENT IN YOUR CHURCH

Phase One:

- Pastor disciples key men/men's director using Maximized Manhood system.

- Launch creates momentum among men

- Church becomes more attractive to hold men who visit

- Families grow stronger

- Men increase bond to pastor

Phase Two:

- Men/men's director teach other men within the church

- Increased tithing and giving by men

- Decreased number of families in crisis

- Increased mentoring of teens and children

- Increase of male volunteers

- Faster assimilation for men visitors - clear path for pastor to connect with new men

- Men pray regularly for pastor

Phase Three:

- Men teach other men outside the church and bring them to Christ

- Increased male population and attraction to a visiting man, seeing a place he belongs

- Stronger, better-attended community outreaches

- Men are loyal to and support pastor

This system enables the pastor to successfully train key leaders, create momentum, build a church that attracts and holds men who visit, and disciple strong men.

Churches may conduct men's ministry entirely a free of charge! Learn how by calling 817-437-4888.

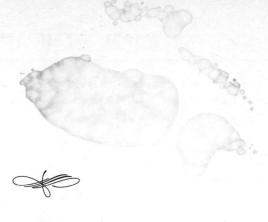

CONTACT
MAJORING IN MEN® CURRICULUM
817-437-4888
admin@ChristianMensNetwork.com

Christian Men's Network
P.O. Box 93478
Southlake, TX 76092

Great discounts available.

Start your discipleship TODAY!

Call today for group discounts
and coaching opportunities.

FREE DVD!
Send your name and address to:
office@ChristianMensNetwork.com
We'll send you a FREE full-length DVD
with ministry for men.
(Limit one per person.)

ABOUT THE AUTHOR

Edwin Louis Cole mentored hundreds of thousands of people through challenging events and powerful books that have become the most widely-used Christian men's resources in the world. He is known for pithy statements and a confrontational style that demanded social responsibility and family leadership.

After serving as a pastor, evangelist, and Christian television pioneer, and at an age when most men were retiring, he followed his greatest passion—to lead men into Christlikeness, which he called "real manhood."

Ed Cole was a real man through and through. A loving son to earthly parents and the heavenly Father. Devoted husband to the "loveliest lady in the land," Nancy Corbett Cole. Dedicated father to three and, over the years, accepting the role of "father" to thousands. A reader, a thinker, a visionary. A man who made mistakes, learned lessons, then shared the wealth of his wisdom with men around the world. The Christian Men's Network he founded in 1977 is still a vibrant, global ministry. Unquestionably, he was the greatest men's minister of his generation.

Facebook.com/EdwinLouisCole